THE MARKETS OF ASIA PACIFIC: INDONESIA

The Asia Pacific Centre is the London-based associate of The Survey Research Group. SRG consists of market research companies in Hong Kong, Singapore, Philippines, Malaysia, Indonesia, Thailand and Australia.

The Asia Pacific Centre Ltd
2-6 Camden High Street
London NW1 OJH

Telephone: 388 5021   Telex: 887560

THE MARKETS OF ASIA/PACIFIC
INDONESIA

The Asia Pacific Centre

Facts On File, Inc.

460 Park Avenue South,
New York, N.Y. 10016

Copyright © 1981 by the Asia Pacific Centre Limited

Published in the United Kingdom in 1981 by Gower Publishing Company Limited, Croft Road, Aldershot, Hampshire, GU11 3HR, England.

Published in the United States of America in 1981 by Facts on File, Inc., 460 Park Avenue South, New York, N.Y. 10016.

Library of Congress Cataloging in Publication Data

Main entry under title:

The Markets of Asia Pacific: INDONESIA

   Includes index.
   1. Indonesia — Economic conditions — 1945.
   2. Indonesia — Commerce. I. Asia Pacific Centre.
HC447.M354   330.9598'038   81-3239
ISBN 0-87196-587-9   AACR2

Printed in Great Britain

Contents

vii

LIST OF TABLES

Foreword

'THE MARKETS OF ASIA PACIFIC' SERIES

The series of books under the title 'The Markets of Asia Pacific' is designed to provide an overview of some of the fastest growing and most dynamic markets in the world. The series will be periodically updated: for most countries, every two years.

An important feature of the series is the release for the first time of the banks of market data owned by the Survey Research Group of companies (SRG). SRG is the largest group of market research companies operating in the Asia Pacific region and heavy investment in syndicated research of their own has led to a considerable amount of new market research information now becoming available. Almost all the SRG information published in this series will not be found in any other published source.

Where SRG information exists, it has considerable depth but it covers by no means all the markets of interest. It has therefore been supplemented by key published statistics from elsewhere. The selection of published statistics has been derived from a search of existing data sources. While it is clearly beyond the scope of the series to quote from all sources found, a listing of titles and locations is included as an important feature in each country book.

In setting a style for the series, emphasis has been put on the provision of hard information rather than interpretative discussion. Wherever possible, however, key points of market development are described in the text. This is designed as a reference series which should provide mostly numeric answers to a range of marketing questions. To facilitate reference a detailed index is provided at the back of the book.

The broad format of each country book is similar but there is some variation in specific content. This is determined by the particular market characteristics of the country and the data that happens to be available.

INDONESIA

This volume draws heavily on surveys conducted by P.T. In-Search Data in recent years. Prior to 1981 this information has not been released for publication in book form and it provides an overview of the main media and consumer markets. We acknowledge the information provided by In-Search Data and their help in identifying key market trends and characteristics.

Most of the remaining information in this book has been derived from Indonesian Government publications and our use of this information is gratefully acknowledged.

Individual sources used for this volume are referenced in the appropriate chapter.

In producing this book the intention has been to provide hard, statistical information across a range of markets and where possible to include new information from SRG company sources.

It is proposed to update this volume on a two-yearly basis. For the interim, the statistics selected should provide the reader with at least a good indication of the main parameters of the markets. Where the latest figures are essential the reader is invited to refer to the Asia Pacific Centre who will either provide them or indicate the best source.

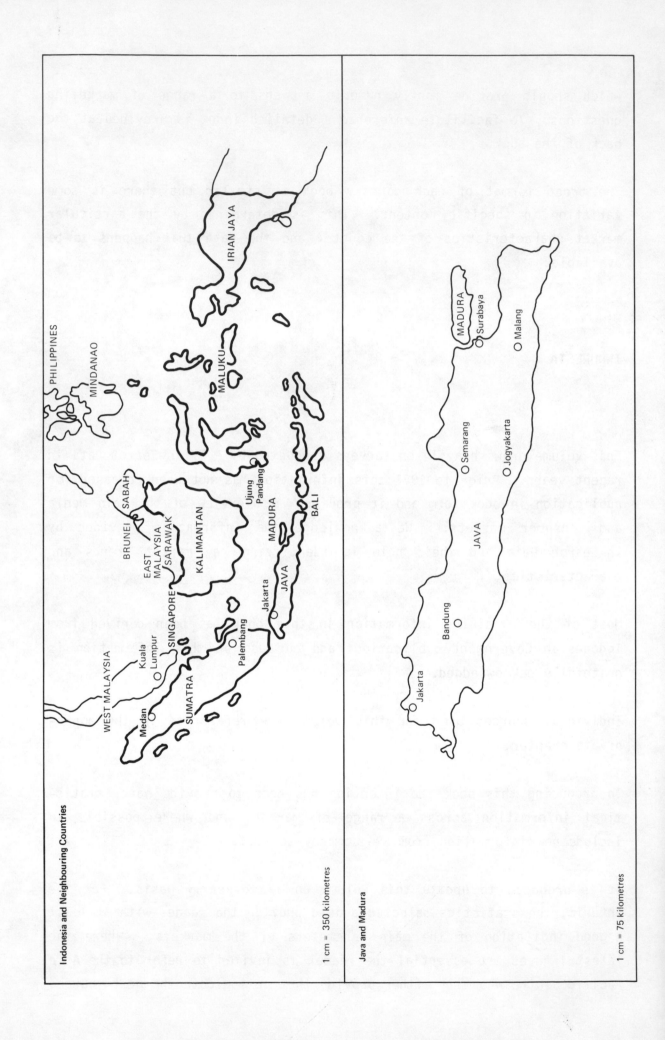

Indonesia and Neighbouring Countries

PHILIPPINES

MINDANAO

IRIAN JAYA

MALUKU

WEST MALAYSIA

Kuala
Lumpur

Medan

SUMATRA

SINGAPORE

BRUNEI

SABAH

EAST
MALAYSIA

SARAWAK

KALIMANTAN

Ujung
Pandang

Palembang

Jakarta

JAVA

MADURA

BALI

1 cm = 350 kilometres

Java and Madura

Jakarta

Bandung

JAVA

Semarang

Jogyakarta

MADURA

Surabaya

Malang

1 cm = 75 kilometres

1 Economic and political background

ECONOMIC BACKGROUND

Indonesia is an archipelago well endowed with natural resources including timber, petroleum, natural gas, fish and a wide variety of strategic minerals, notably nickel, copper, tin and bauxite. Already it is the world's second largest producer of rubber and tin (after Malaysia) and the second largest coconut producer (after the Philippines). Within the Asia Pacific region it is the second largest producer of oil (after China) and the largest exporter.

However with its population of 147 million (and still growing) largely dependent on agriculture and an underdeveloped manufacturing sector Indonesia remains per capita one of the poorest countries in the region. The population growth rate of 2%* adds 3 million new mouths every year, and this is one of the most serious problems facing Indonesia in the future. Although there are some good signs today of economic progress, the country has suffered from long periods of economic mismanagement which, for example, have left it as one of the heaviest **importers** of oil in the region, and even an **importer** of coconut oil and copra. Despite its geographical size, success with higher yielding rice variants and the fact that about 2 in every 3 workers are farmers, Indonesia is unable to feed itself and is the world's largest importer of its staple food, rice.

* National Family Planning Co-ordinating Board estimate at 1981. The 1980 Census shows growth from 1971-80 of 2.34%.

In the post-independence era of President Sukarno, Indonesia failed to build on the economic foundations laid by the Dutch. Sukarno was over-preoccupied with foreign policy and when he was deposed in 1966 Indonesia had an inflation rate of over 600%. In the period since he succeeded Sukarno, President Suharto has pursued a policy of stabilisation with an emphasis on more jobs, more food and a more even distribution of income. Economic development has been pursued through a series of 5 year development plans (Repelitas).

Repelita I began in 1969/70 and stressed the development of industries in the agricultural sector. Repelita II concentrated on the development of industries producing processed raw materials such as wood, leather and minerals. Repelita III, launched in 1979/80 will run to 1983/84. It emphasises the development of industries producing manufactured goods within the broad objective of creating more jobs and a more even spread of development effort throughout the country. Repelita III plans to expand the economy by an average of 6.5% per annum. The fourth plan (starting 1984/85) is expected to feature the development of heavy and machinery industries.

However, the Seventies have not been without their problems for Indonesia. Pertamina - the State oil company - collapsed in 1975 with debts of US$10 billion and it was estimated that large sums of State revenue were dissipated with corruption. Indonesia's small manufacturing sector was run inefficiently, not encouraged to grow sufficiently and improved local food supplies could not keep pace with population growth.

In November 1978 Indonesia implemented a 33.6% devaluation of the Rupiah in a bid to cut back on the consumption of imported goods and to give a boost to export-orientated manufacturing industry as well as generally encouraging foreign investment.

At the end of the decade oil and other commodity prices rose sharply giving Indonesia an unexpected but welcome boost in earnings. At the end of 1979 there was a current account surplus on the balance of payments of US$2.4 billion and a trade surplus of US$8.4 billion.

Although per capita GDP remains low by world standards (c.US$370 in 1979) it has been rising through the latter half of the Seventies at an average of 6.0%.   The percentage of GDP accounted for by the manufacturing sector has been slowly increasing and is planned under Repelita III to average 11% growth per annum.   However, GDP will remain dominated by output from the agriculture/forestry/fishing sector for a considerable time yet.

Table 1 - Distribution of major sectors of GDP by year

(Rp billions at 1973 market prices)

	1975	1976	1977	1978	1979
	%	%	%	%	%
Agriculture, forestry, fishing	36.8	36.1	34.1	33.1	32.2
Mining and quarrying	10.9	11.7	12.2	11.0	10.5
Manufacturing	11.1	11.4	11.5	12.4	12.9
Construction	4.8	4.7	5.2	5.6	5.7
Wholesale and retail trade	17.0	16.6	16.5	16.2	16.4
Transport and communications	4.0	4.2	4.6	5.2	5.6
Banking and financial services	1.3	1.4	1.1	1.7	1.8
Public admin. and defence	7.4	7.3	8.0	8.1	8.0
Services	3.6	3.5	3.3	3.1	3.1
Other	3.1	3.1	3.4	3.6	3.7

Source :- Central Bureau of Statistics

An important question for Indonesia now is the extent to which it can use its short term oil wealth to get industries moving.   In some respects short term money will not solve the fundamental problems.

Greater industrialisation will put greater pressure on an administration which is already unwieldy but inadequate, whose efficiency is impaired with arbitrary taxation, pay-offs, customs delays and inefficient bureaucracy. There is abundant labour, but it is largely unskilled. A shortage of good local management leads to a danger of encouraging capital rather than labour intensive industry. This will not help unemployment and under-employment which unofficial estimates already put at 30% - 40% of the workforce.

The high rate of inflation of the Sixties was under reasonable control by the end of the decade (c.12% in 1970). Price increases surged again to close to 20% by the mid Seventies but came down to a low of 8.6% in 1978. The 1978 Rupiah devaluation and a Government set rise in the domestic prices of certain key commodities (to curb growth in subsidies) brought inflation up to 24.4% in 1979. It has been declining fairly steadily since mid-1979 and at August 1980 was at an annual rate of 15.5% (Consumer Price Index - 17 cities).

With an undercurrent of social unrest, the Government is attempting fair distribution of wealth, and has introduced measures beneficial to the indigenous Indonesians -'Pribumi'. For example, all new companies must be 20% Pribumi-owned at the outset and at least 51% owned within 10 years. Pribumi are also favoured in the awarding of contracts. However, it has been estimated that Indonesia's 2-3 million of Chinese descent control 80%-90% of trade and there is resentment that many of the incentives designed to move the economy are benefitting the Chinese. The situation becomes less clear as the Chinese retreat behind nominal Pribumi company heads.

Corruption is a continuing problem for Indonesia. In 1978 the Attorney General told an investigating commission that Rp 30 billion had been embezzled from State funds during the year. Others have estimated that up to 30% of State funds are lost through 'leakage'. A vigorous anti-corruption campaign has been in force since mid-1977 but there is widespread business scepticism that such an ingrained practice can be overcome.

Foreign overseas companies - led by Japan - are still investing heavily in Indonesia. By March 1980 there were 786 licensed foreign investment projects throughout the country, which, excluding those in oil and gas, amounted to a total investment of US$8,437 million.

Table 2 - Distribution of investment funds in approved
projects (1967 - 1980 March)

	Total Investment
	%
Japan	37.7
USA	8.4
Hong Kong	9.7
Philippines	3.7
Europe	13.6
Others	26.9

Source :- Investment Co-ordinating Board

The decade ended with Indonesia in a strong financial position thanks to oil revenues and making definite efforts to encourage investment - particularly in labour intensive, higher technology industries. In broad terms, three areas of development have been put forward as good prospects:-

- garments and electronics assembly, because of the high ratio of productivity to labour costs
- industries processing local agricultural products such as palm oil and timber
- industries based on the country's abundant gas such as urea and cement.

However, for many commentators it is still too early to say whether planned investment will meet its targets with the background of fundamental problems outlined above. The budget for the financial year 1980/81 was planned at about US$16.8 billion - over 50% up on the previous year.

48% of the budget expenditure was taken up by development expenditure. Oil revenue was expected to increase by 92% and non-oil by only 8%. Oil revenue was expected to constitute 71% of total revenue.

POLITICAL BACKGROUND

Indonesia is a republic whose Constitution vests highest authority in the People's Consultative Assembly (MPR). There are four independent entities: The President, The House of People's Representatives, The Supreme Audit Board and The Supreme Court. There is also The Supreme Advisory Council which acts as adviser and consultant to the President.

The MPR determines general government policy and elects the President - who is Head of Government - and the Vice-President. The present MPR has 230 representatives from the Armed Forces, 130 from the Regional Delegates Faction, 42 from the Development Democracy Faction, 392 from the Development Functional Faction and 126 from the Development United.

Parliamentary elections are due early in 1982 and Presidential elections in 1983. The strengthening of the economy at the end of the Seventies has had an insignificant effect on Indonesia's social problems. However, opposition to the present regime is disunited and is unlikely to offer any serious challenge to the Government.

Communism is seen by the Government as a latent threat which could emerge if the needs of the people are not met. This reinforces the Government objective of developing the rural sector. The Armed Forces are likely to retain their role in Government for the foreseeable future and the short term prognosis is generally agreed to be one of political stability.

Table 3 - Economic Indicators

	1975	1978	1979	1980
Gross Domestic Product at current market- prices (GDP)-(in US$ million)	30,292	37,001	55,500	N.A
GDP per capita at current market prices - (in US$)	224	255	370	N.A
Real GDP growth (%) -	5.0	6.8	4.9	7.0
Balance of Trade (US$ million) -	2,332	4,953	8,354	11,270
Balance of payments (Current account balance - US$ million) -	- 854	-1,155	+2,370	N.A
Money supply (% growth rate) (currency in circ. + demand deposits) -	33.3	24.0	29.0	N.A
Inflation rate (CPI % growth) -	19.0	8.6	24.4	15.0
Exchange rate at period end (Rp per US$)-	415	625	627	N.A

Source :- Bank Indonesia, Central Bureau of Statistics,
            Ministry of Finance, Malaysia

Table 4 - Annual changes in real GNP/GDP growth for selected countries (1976-79)

	1976	1977	1978	1979*
Percentage growth in GNP/GDP				
- Total OECD	5.2	3.7	3.7	3.4
- USA	5.8	4.9	4.4	2.3
- Japan	6.0	5.4	5.9	6.0
- West Germany	5.6	2.6	3.5	4.4
- France	5.6	3.0	3.5	3.7
- United Kingdom	2.6	2.0	3.4	1.1
- ASEAN				
- **Indonesia**	**6.9**	**7.4**	**6.8**	**4.9**
- Malaysia	11.6	7.7	7.5	8.5
- Philippines	6.1	6.1	6.3	5.8
- Singapore	7.2	7.8	8.6	9.3
- Thailand	9.3	7.3	11.7	6.7
- Other				
- Hong Kong	16.7	9.8	10.0	11.5
- South Korea	15.1	10.3	11.6	3.5
- Taiwan	11.5	8.5	12.8	8.0

Sources :- OECD

Official Country Reports

Central Bureau of Statistics

Ministry of Finance, Malaysia

Singapore 1980 Budget Report

National Economic and Social Development Board, Bangkok

Table 5 - Annual changes in consumer prices for selected countries (1976-79)

	1976	1977	1978	1979
Percentage growth in GNP/GDP				
- Total OECD	8.6	8.7	7.9	9.9
- USA	5.8	6.5	7.7	9.0
- Japan	9.3	8.1	3.8	3.3
- West Germany	4.5	3.9	2.6	4.3
- France	9.6	9.4	9.1	10.7
- United Kingdom	16.5	15.9	8.3	12.2
- ASEAN				
- Indonesia	**19.8**	**11.0**	**8.6**	**24.4**
- Malaysia	2.6	4.7	4.9	3.6
- Philippines	6.2	7.9	7.6	18.8
- Singapore	-1.9	3.2	4.8	4.0
- Thailand	4.2	7.2	8.0	15.0
- Other				
- Hong Kong	3.4	5.8	5.0	11.6
- South Korea	15.4	10.1	14.4	18.3
- Taiwan	2.5	7.0	5.8	10.3

Sources :- OECD
        Official Country Reports
        Ministry of Finance, Malaysia
        Singapore 1980 Budget Report
        Bangkok Bank
        Hong Kong Census and Statistics Department

2 The people

Indonesia is the world's largest archipelago consisting of 13,667 islands spread across the equator, of which just under half are inhabited. The total land area is approximately 1.9 million square kilometres. The largest islands are Sumatra, Kalimantan (Indonesian Borneo), Java, Sulawesi and Irianjaya (West Irian).

First figures from the 1980 population Census put the total population at 147 million making it the fifth most populous country in the world. The growth rate in the period 1971-80 has been 2.34%. The male to female ratio at 1980 was 988:1000.

**Table 6 - Population profile :- sex and age
        by urban/rural**

	Total	Urban	Rural
('000s)	126,093*	23,330	102,763
	%	%	%
Male	49	50	49
Female	51	50	51
0-14yrs	42	41	42
15-24	19	22	18
25-34	13	13	13
35-49	16	15	16
50+	10	9	11

* Based on 1976 Intercensal Population Survey
Source :- Central Bureau of Statistics - Intercensal Population Survey-

Population Distribution By Age

Age

NO.('000s)

Age	NO.('000s)
70+	2,391
65-69	2,107
60-64	3,016
55-59	3,970
50-54	4,985
45-49	6,103
40-44	7,510
35-39	7,452
30-34	7,844
25-29	10,888
20-24	13,369
15-19	15,852
10-14	17,811
5- 9	18,530
0- 4	20,352

Source :- Central Bureau of Statistics - population projection 1980

The population growth rate represents a major problem for Indonesia with the Seventies alone having seen an increase of some 28 million. Family planning has been actively supported by the Government since 1967 and since then the numbers of family planning clinics and fieldworkers has been growing rapidly.

However, while the numbers of acceptors of birth control have been increasing they still represent a minority of the population (an estimated 4.7 million permanent acceptors at the end of Repelita II) and there is still a great deal of work to be done :- particularly in the rural areas and the outer islands, (The target of permanent acceptors for the end of Repelita III is 9.5 million). Promotional campaigns are aimed at encouraging parents to limit families to two children. Yet even if Indonesia can achieve a two child family average by the year 2000, zero population growth can still not occur until the population is approximately 330 million.

With the current rates of growth the population is estimated to reach 167 million by 1985 so that even in the short term there will be population pressures. For example, by that time there will be well over 700 people per square kilometre on the island of Java.

A result of such fast growth in the numbers of people is a heavy bulge at the young end of the population age distributon. This is demonstrated in the figure above both numerically and visually. 60% of the entire population was under the age of 25 at 1980.

One of the most complex aspects of the Indonesian people is their sheer diversity. Indeed their national motto reflects this feature (Bhinneka Tunggal Ika - Unity in diversity). Over three hundred ethnic groups are represented in the archipelago, speaking over two hundred and fifty different languages and dialects. However, over 90% of the population derive from one ethnic group, the Malays and there is a single national language - Bahasa Indonesia - which is widely understood (see below). An estimated 9% of the population are of Chinese origin and although in such a minority are particularly important in business and commerce.

There have been a number of important influences on Indonesian social and religious behaviour which are manifest in fairly strong regional differences today. In the early centuries A.D., Indian traders brought the Hindu and Buddhist religions to Sumatra. Around the fifteenth century Islam spread across from Malacca and with the greater penetration of Islamic traders the population became predominantly Muslim. Today the only Hindu communities are in Bali and Lombok, and over 90% of people claim to be Muslim. However, the religion has been adapted to suit the existing Indonesian culture and is not always followed as strictly as in Malaysia and parts of the Arab world.

Western influence, including the Christian religion, was brought to Indonesia by the Dutch who traded in spices from the Moluccas, and effectively colonised Indonesia - known then as the Netherlands East Indies - in the seventeenth century. Today there remains a strong Christian element in the Moluccas, on the Northern peninsula of Sulawesi and in Sumatra. A particularly important aspect of the presence of the Dutch was their development of Java as the centre of clerical administration which brought foreign enterprise, capital and the development of an economic infrastructure.

These sources of influence have been greater in the more developed trading areas; the hinterland and more remote islands have been relatively unaffected. The result is a syncretism in which the modern day culture has developed from successive layers of influence and yet retained something of its original character.

POPULATION DISTRIBUTION

Indonesia's population explosion has created problems of providing enough food, which has in turn led to migration and a heavy clustering in the more fertile land zones. At present more than 60% of the population is crammed into the relatively fertile island of Java which has less than 10% of the total land space. Java benefits from its rich volcanic and alluvial soils, ample rain, a gentle topography and Dutch initiated drainage systems. Most of Indonesia's rice is grown on Java for which an early name was the 'Rice Island'. In terms of population the principal cities are Jakarta, Surabaya, Bandung and Semarang. At present there are just over 600 people per square kilometre of Java.

By comparison, Sumatra has only 18% of the population living in 25% of Indonesia's total land space, giving a population density of 50 people per square kilometre. In general the terrain is much less hospitable for agriculture than Java although estates (tobacco, rubber, palm oil) are more common particularly along the Northeast coast. In addition, Sumatra has important mineral resources (e.g. oil, tin, bauxite).

The largest cities are Medan and Palembang: the former has a noticeably better-off population (see below) than the other main Indonesian cities.

Sulawesi, formerly called the Celebes, has 7% of the population: patchily distributed. There is significant rice cultivation on the northern peninsula and some commercial crops (cloves, coffee, copra) but Sulawesi is heavily dependent on the sea for its subsistence. The major cities are Ujung Pandang and Manado.

Kalimantan is sparsely populated with about 5% of the population and is one of the important islands in the Government's plans to redistribute the population. The terrain does not suit it for agricultural development (although oil and timber will provide a future economic base) and historically it missed out on the major trade routes and consequent 'trader' development.

MIGRATION

While Indonesia's population has grown in the more fertile regions where it can feed itself, a secondary phenomenon has been migration (natural migration as opposed to Government resettlement in which 104,000 families were resettled in less populous areas under Repelitas I and II and 500,000 families are planned to be resettled under Repelita III) from rural to urban centres. This may be either permanent or temporary migration when farmers use the period between crops to earn cash income in the urban areas (e.g by driving a bejak or

by hawking). THe following figures demonstrate that only about half of
all adults in the major towns were born in them, and that in Java the
larger towns of Jakarta and Surabaya have particularly high proportions
of non-native adults.

Table 7 - Place of birth in relation to town of residence

	Total Adults	Jakar -ta	Ban- dung	Sema- rang	Solo	Jogya- karta	Sura- baya	Malang	Medan	Palem -bang	Ujung Pandang
('000s)	8,787	3,753	795	599	292	255	1,323	291	675	407	397
	%	%	%	%	%	%	%	%	%	%	%
Birthplace											
- Town of Interview	49	48	53	55	58	67	38	58	49	52	47
- Other	51	52	47	45	42	33	62	42	51	48	53

Source :- In-Search Media Index Survey - 1979

The more industrialised cities have been favoured for migration (for
example over the more historical cultural centres of Solo and
Jogyakarta) and this has led to a varied age distribution across the
main towns. Both age and the levels of household expenditure for 10
major cities are reflected below.

Table 8 - Adult age and socio economic status by city

	Total Adults	Jakar -ta	Ban- dung	Sema- rang	Solo	Jogya- karta	Sura- baya	Malang	Medan	Palem -bang	Ujung Pandang
('000s)	8,787	3,753	795	599	292	255	1,323	291	675	407	397
Age:-	%	%	%	%	%	%	%	%	%	%	%
- 15-19 yrs	21	20	19	20	21	18	21	18	24	24	20
- 20-24	18	18	20	14	14	18	17	15	20	19	20
- 25-29	14	15	12	13	12	11	12	12	14	14	13
- 30-34	10	11	11	9	8	9	9	10	7	9	12
- 35-39	10	11	9	10	7	8	9	10	8	7	9
- 40-49	14	13	14	17	17	13	16	16	13	14	15
- 50+	14	13	15	18	20	23	15	19	14	14	13
Live in household with monthly expenditure											
-A1-RP150,000+	3	4	5	1	2	1	2	2	5	1	1
-A2-RP 75,001-150,000	15	18	16	9	8	11	15	5	21	8	7
- B-RP 50,001- 75,000	15	17	12	11	12	13	17	10	20	14	10
- C-RP 30,001- 50,000	26	29	22	19	22	22	25	18	32	32	22
- D-RP 20,001- 30,000	22	21	26	23	22	26	21	21	15	29	31
- E-RP 10,001- 20,000	14	9	16	27	24	18	15	26	6	14	22
- F-RP 10,000 and less	4	2	3	11	10	9	5	20	1	3	8

Source :- In-Search Media Index Survey - 1979

INDONESIA'S POVERTY

The levels of household expenditure shown in the table above reflect the low levels of income of urban dwellers and these figures will be higher than those in the rural areas. In 1979 an In-Search survey of households in Jakarta estimated the average household expenditure at approximately Rp 41,000 per month. This figure corresponds with the Government's National Socio-Economic Survey of 1976 in which average monthly **per capita** expenditure for urban dwellers was estimated at Rp 6,775 (or Rp 37,000 per household if an average household size of 5.5 is taken).

The table below summarizes the main expenditure categories from the Government survey. A significant feature is that 69% of total per capita expenditure went on **food** with 29% on cereals (mainly rice).

Although cigarettes are not expensive in Indonesia, more money was spent on tobacco/betel nut than on meat or clothing and footwear. A marginally higher proportion of rural expenditure was going on tobacco/betel nut than urban expenditure.

The main differences between urban and rural spending are largely to be expected with relatively more rural expenditure going on the basic subsistence items such as rice and less on housing and related utilities. In gross terms urban expenditure was 73% higher than rural expenditure.

It is a comment on the style of rural life that despite having less money to spend overall, the rural dwellers still outspent the urban dwellers on a per capita basis for parties and ceremonies.

Table 9 - Average per capita monthly expenditure
- Rupiah and percentage - by urban/rural

	Total Indonesia		Urban		Rural	
	Rp	%	Rp	%	Rp	%
Food						
Cereals/ products	1,303	29.4	1,317	19.4	1,300	33.2
Cassava/ products	117	2.7	43	.6	134	3.4
Fish and other sea food	285	6.4	419	6.2	255	6.5
Meat	153	3.5	312	4.6	118	3.0
Eggs, milk and milk prods.	79	1.8	225	3.3	47	1.2
Vegetables	251	5.7	342	5.1	231	5.9
Nuts	101	2.3	168	2.5	87	2.2
Fruit	101	2.6	176	2.6	101	2.6
Miscellaneous	442	10.0	565	8.4	415	10.6
Prepared Food	175	4.0	387	5.7	128	3.3
Alcoholic beverages	8	.2	15	.2	7	.2
Tobacco/ betel nut	238	5.4	355	5.2	212	5.4
Non-food						
Housing/fuel/light/water	446	10.1	1,130	16.7	295	7.6
Miscellaneous goods and services	267	6.0	739	10.9	163	4.2
Clothing/footwear	221	5.0	322	4.8	199	5.1
Durable goods	114	2.6	146	2.2	107	2.7
Consumption taxes/ Insurance premiums	37	.8	52	.8	34	.9
Parties and ceremonies	75	1.7	64	1.0	78	2.0
Total	**4,426**	**100.0**	**6,775**	**100.0**	**3,909**	**100.0**

Source :- National Socio-Economic Survey:- Jan-Dec 1976

The low levels of income are essentially a function of the large agricultural base of the Indonesian economy. The figures below are taken from the 1976 Inter-Censal Population Survey and serve to show the very high proportion of the working population engaged in the agricultural sector: (where almost all are Petani - small holding farmers).

Table 10 - Profile of the working population

Total working population aged 10 or over	100%
Occupation category	
- Agriculture	66.0%
- Mining	*
- Manufacturing	6.7%
- Electricity	*
- Construction	2.0%
- Trade	11.7%
- Transportation	2.1%
- Financing	*
- Services	9.6%
- Other	1.6%

Source :- Central Bureau of Statistics - 1976 Inter-censal
Population Survey

Socio-demographic profile of main conurbations

This section focuses attention on the socio-economic profile of 10 main conurbations of Indonesia and is largely dependent on information from In-Search Data. These cities have been chosen by In-Search because of their size, relative wealth and consequent importance to those marketing consumer goods and services. The population of the ten cities shown represents 75% of the urban population in Indonesia.

14% of the adult population were in white collar jobs in 1979 and 19% in blue collar jobs. Blue collar workers were more likely to be found in Semarang and Malang which both had relatively high proportions of working women. Over the 10 urban areas, 23% of adult women were working compared with 53% who were housewives, 12% students and 12% unemployed.

Table 11 - Adult occupation by city

	Total Adults	Jakar -ta	Ban- dung	Sema- rang	Solo	Jogya- karta	Sura- baya	Malang	Medan	Palem -bang	Ujung Pandang
('000s)	8,787	3,753	795	599	292	255	1,323	291	675	407	397
	%	%	%	%	%	%	%	%	%	%	%
Professional/exec	1	1	1	*		*	1	1	1	*	1
Supervisor	1	1	1	1	*	2	1	1	1	1	1
Clerical staff	12	12	10	11	11	14	17	10	11	9	10
Self employed	8	8	9	9	12	11	9	12	8	8	5
Skilled/semi-skilled	5	5	6	6	4	6	5	8	5	6	5
Labourers	12	10	10	19	20	13	17	17	6	8	8
Farmers/fishermen	2	2	1	4	1	*	*	1	2	2	3
Students	16	14	16	14	16	23	16	16	18	17	19
Pensioners	2	1	2	2	3	3	2	3	2	2	2
Unemployed	12	12	8	11	9	9	10	9	18	15	12
Housewives	30	34	35	24	23	18	22	20	28	30	33

Source :- In-Search Media Index Survey - 1979

19% of adults had no formal schooling with a further 17% not finishing primary school.   Women were less well-educated with 44% not finishing primary compared with 24% for men.   Only 4% of men and 1% of women had any tertiary education whether vocational or academic.

The literacy figures shown in the table below depend on an ability to read two fairly simple test sentences.   In these terms urban comprehension of the national language is high (although it evolved from a minority Sumatran Malay dialect).   The English literacy figures are particularly high in the two university towns of Bandung and Jogyakarta (the latter is also an historic cultural centre for visitors - and has the highest level of Dutch literacy of the two towns).   Bearing in mind that Indonesia was a Dutch colony for many years the predominance of English literacy over Dutch is remarkable and emphasises that only a small minority of the present population were alive at that time.

Table 12 - Education and literacy by city

	Total Adults	Jakar -ta	Ban- dung	Sema- rang	Solo	Jogya- karta	Sura- baya	Malang	Medan	Palem -bang	Ujung Pandang
('000s)	8,787	3,753	795	599	292	255	1,323	291	675	407	397
	%	%	%	%	%	%	%	%	%	%	%
Education :-											
-No formal schooling	19	20	13	27	23	17	18	23	9	17	21
-Not finish SD(Primary)	17	16	16	18	16	13	17	20	16	23	19
-SD	26	27	31	21	21	20	25	24	31	26	23
-SLP (Junior secondary)	20	19	21	19	22	21	21	17	23	19	19
-SLA (High school)	15	15	16	13	15	20	17	13	18	13	15
-Academy(more vocational	2	2	2	2	3	8	1	2	2	1	3
-University	1	1	1	1	*	2	1	1	*	1	*
Able to read test sentence in :-											
-Bahasa Indonesia	82	81	88	72	77	82	81	76	91	87	78
-English	24	22	34	28	25	42	23	20	24	14	15
-Chinese	3	2	3	2	2	1	5	2	8	5	3
-Dutch	4	4	6	3	4	9	6	3	3	2	2

Source :- In-Search Media Index Survey - 1979

The large demographic variations in education and literacy are highlighted in the following table which specifically concerns the largest town - Jakarta. Besides the higher educational levels for men, the key feature is the much lower education level and literacy for those people aged 40 years or over (although Dutch literacy is highest for those 40+).

Table 13 - Education level and literacy by sex and age (Jakarta)

	Total Adults	Male	Female	15-19	20-29	30-39	40+
('000s)	3,750	1,664	2.087	710	1,348	804	888
	%	%	%	%	%	%	%
Education :-							
- No formal schooling	20	11	27	9	10	17	40
- Not finish SD(primary)	16	13	18	16	13	17	17
- SD	27	29	24	33	27	26	23
- SLP (Junior secondary)	19	24	16	36	18	18	10
- SLA (High school)	15	18	12	6	27	18	6
- Academy(more vocational)	2	4	1		4	2	2
- University	1	1	1		*	2	1
Able to read test sentence in :-							
- Bahasa Indonesia	81	89	75	91	90	84	62
- English	22	28	17	26	27	22	15
- Chinese	2	2	2	1	1	3	3
- Dutch	4	5	4	1	2	5	10

Source :- In-Search Media Index Survey - 1979

Living conditions are variable across the 10 cities. Detached/semi-detached houses are the most common form of dwelling for all the cities with the cities of Sumatra more likely than others to have terrace blocks as the second most common dwelling type. At the poorest extreme a solid minority live in attap / bamboo shacks.

About half of all dwellings have brick walls, and about one third are made of wood. Tile floors are common in Java but not elsewhere. An interesting feature of home development is that the building may well take place over time as money becomes available. It would not be uncommon to put up external walls and then add floors, ceiling, divisions at later stages.

The provision of electricity is increasing but remains at a relatively low level. In 1977 In-Search estimated only 19% of adults in Jakarta had electricity in their homes. By 1979 the Jakarta estimate was 44% and it is still quite common to see television sets being run off car batteries.

Less than 1 in 5 urban homes has running water, although the cities of Sumatra are better provided in this respect. Again the situation improved significantly between 1977 and 1979 (e.g. the piped water penetration in Jakarta more than doubled).

Only 3% of adults have a telephone in the home.

Table 14 describes households across the 10 cities. As well as describing physical characteristics it shows the origins of household members. Medan and Surabaya are cities of relative Chinese strength although in no city do the Chinese account for more than one in five households.

Table 14 - Household description by city

	Jakar-ta	Ban-dung	Sema-rang	Solo	Jogya-Karta	Sura-baya	Malang	Medan	Palem-bang	Ujung Pandang
('000s)	3,753	795	599	292	255	1,323	291	675	407	397
	%	%	%	%	%	%	%	%	%	%
Type of house:-										
- Detached/semi	68	86	89	83	88	90	83	72	79	80
- Terrace/bars	10	5	5	1	*	3	1	21	12	2
- Shop house	1	2	2	2	*	1	1	2	*	4
- Flat/apartment	1					*		2	*	
- Attap/bamboo shack	21	8	4	14	11	6	14	3	8	14
Type of building										
- Brick walls	57	67	42	49	59	70	72	43	21	39
- Wood	33	26	54	19	11	21	5	53	78	45
- Metal/zinc	*		*			*		*	*	1
- Bamboo	10	7	4	31	30	9	23	3		15
- Other		*		1		*			*	
Facilities										
- Tile floor	59	72	45	49	48	68	70	17	18	17
- Electricity	44	73	41	49	55	73	51	52	59	56
- Running water	15	25	15	13	19	38	17	26	37	9
- Telephone	3	4	4	5	2	6	2	6	1	3
Origin										
- Indigenous	91	92	87	91	96	86	96	82	91	92
- Chinese descent	9	8	12	8	4	14	3	16	8	7
- Other Asian descent			*	1	*	*		2	2	
- Other	*		*	*		*	*	*		*

Source :- In-Search Media Index Survey - 1979

The information above is based on a survey of people. However, a certain amount of information is available from In-Search based on a 1979 survey of households in Jakarta. As a further indication of the level of prosperity of Jakarta homes the following figures have been extracted.

Table 15 - Household ownership of durable goods (Jakarta)

	Total Jakarta Households
	('000s) 1,252
	%
Possession of durable goods	
- Bicycle	18
- Sewing machine	53
- Radio	61
- Cassette/Radio cassette	46
- Black and white TV	39
- Colour TV	1
- Air-conditioner	1
- Stereo set	5
- Refrigerator	11
- Company/ Govt. car	2
- Private car	5
- Motor bike	18

Source :- In-Search Household Survey - 1979

Information derived from the same survey shows that only 16% of all Jakarta households have more than 100 square metres of space and only 56% have glass windows.

The final table in this section concerns Jakarta again and will be relevant to those marketing products for children or mothers. 80% of Jakarta homes have children in them and more than a third have an infant under two years of age. The figures for the other main towns are broadly similar.

Table 16 - Presence of children by household expenditure - (Jakarta)

	Total Adults	Household Expenditure in Rp'000					
		150+(A1)	75-150(A2)	50-75(B)	30-50(C)	20-30(D)	-20(E)
('000s)	3,750	148	668	624	1,074	815	422
	%	%	%	%	%	%	%
Living in household with one or more children aged :-							
- Less than 12 months	13	14	8	11	14	16	12
- 12 - 23 months	22	5	11	11	13	14	9
- 2 - 4 years	38	27	31	39	42	41	35
- 5 - 14 years	67	59	73	78	67	62	53
Any less than 15 years	80	70	83	85	82	80	66

Source :- In-Search Media Index Survey - 1979

3 Consumer markets — non durables

In this and the following section the objective is to provide a brief summary of the main consumer markets :- i.e. those in which the advertising and research expenditure tends to be high. For each market covered, size - in terms of numbers of consumers - is given together with an indication of the leading brands.

The data covers 10 main conurbations and breakdowns are provided for each. Where possible, similar information for Jakarta in 1977 is used to reflect market trends. Jakarta is also taken as the example for demographic fluctuations in the market.

All of the statistics in these two sections have been culled from the In-Search Marketing Index which took place between September 5th and November 5th 1979. In other words it reflects the market situation at the **end** of 1979.

With its population of 147 million Indonesia represents an enormous market place and even where market penetrations are still low, in gross terms the numbers can be large when compared with Indonesia's Asian neighbours. For example a product consumed by just 4% of the total population would have a market larger than the entire Hong Kong population and more than twice the population of Singapore.

Despite the low earnings of Indonesian families, a striking feature of the market is the potential which exists for consumer goods. With increased oil revenues and the Government's programmes to redistribute wealth more evenly, the growth that is already emerging in certain markets should continue, and new sectors are likely to open up.

Even today, it is noticeable that there are markets of relatively low penetration where 'users' are not very different from 'non-users' in terms of household expenditure. These are markets where growth should be possible even without marked increases in consumer wealth.

In terms of market potential, one should not ignore the bulge in the population, currently below the 15 year level, which will soon start to move into the age groups of personal and household expenditure. At the same time they will be bringing with them higher standards of education and literacy and a greater exposure to Western influences.

Finally, there will be a growth in the population over the next half-decade alone of some 16 million people.

Looking ahead the markets will be there for development: the problems will lie in the marketing methods used to develop them. Apart from the problems of researching and understanding Indonesia's diversity there will be difficulties in the distribution of goods and in the creation and execution of promotional campaigns :- these are considered in subsequent chapters. However, those companies who have pursued their commitment to Indonesia through difficult conditions are now beginning to reap considerable benefit as some of the figures below will indicate.

Any company about to involve itself in the consumer markets of Indonesia will need to investigate the administrative, social and cultural back-grounds which might prevail. It is beyond the scope of this chapter to provide an all embracing analysis of possible market influences but some important areas for consideration are :-

- religious taboos :- relevant for certain foods and alcoholic beverages,

- regional variability in market performance :- as the market summaries below will show, regional differences can be quite extreme. This could be a function of ethnic or socio-demographic differences within the population or simply a matter of differential product distribution,

- Indonesian concern for health:- hypochondria is too strong
  term to use but the people evidence considerable concern over
  health and the pharmaceutical sector is a particularly
  important part of the consumer goods market. The traditional
  herbal remedies -'jamus'- are a good indication of this
  market strength,

- the importance of packaging :- particularly in relation to
  crowded shop displays and the good possibility of a long
  shelf life. The low level of English literacy is an
  important factor,

- difficulty in getting enough advertising cover for certain
  market segments, with the implication that each piece of
  advertising has to work that much harder,

- difficulty in controlling distribution,

- a certain amount of racial prejudice from the market mass of
  indigenous Indonesians.

Analgesics
Table 17 - Market summary by city

	Total Adults	Jakar -ta	Ban- dung	Sema- rang	Solo	Jogya- karta	Sura- baya	Malang	Medan	Palem -bang	Ujung Pandang
('000s)	8,787	3,753	795	599	292	255	1,323	291	675	407	397
	%	%	%	%	%	%	%	%	%	%	%
Market Penetration											
- sometimes take	80	81	84	73	67	74	80	75	77	83	87

Leading Brands :- Bodrex, Bintang Tujuh, Inza

Source :- In-Search Marketing Index - 1979

Market comment :- A highly fragmented but extremely large market in which small unit purchases of just one or two tablets are frequently made. No growth in Jakarta market penetration since 1977. The profile of users is very similar to the adult profile as a whole.

Sweetened Condensed Milk
Table 18 - Market summary by city

	Total Adults	Jakar -ta	Ban- dung	Sema- rang	Solo	Jogya- karta	Sura- baya	Malang	Medan	Palem -bang	Ujung Pandang
('000s)	8,787	3,753	795	599	292	255	1,323	291	675	407	397
	%	%	%	%	%	%	%	%	%	%	%
Market Penetration											
- sometimes take	59	65	65	31	34	58	39	31	70	86	85

Leading Brands :- Frisian Flag, Indo Milk, Nestle

Source :- In-Search Marketing Index - 1979

Market Comment :- Apart from the sizeable adult consumption, sweetened condensed milk is popular with children. No growth in Jakarta market penetration since 1977. The profile of users is very similar to the adult profile as a whole.

Health Food Drinks
Table 19 - Market summary by city

	Total Adults	Jakar -ta	Ban- dung	Sema- rang	Solo	Jogya- karta	Sura- baya	Malang	Medan	Palem -bang	Ujung Pandang
('000s)	8,787	3,753	795	599	292	255	1,323	291	675	407	397
	%	%	%	%	%	%	%	%	%	%	%
Market Penetration											
- sometimes take	9	10	14	2	4	7	8	4	21	8	20

Leading Brands :- Ovaltine, Milo, Malcoa

Source :- In-Search Marketing Index - 1979

Market comment :- A minority market but one with some growth :- Jakarta penetration up from 7% in 1977. Consumption is found disproportionately with those from higher income homes and the 15-19 year olds.

Powdered Milk
Table 20 - Market summary by city

	Total Adults	Jakar -ta	Ban- dung	Sema- rang	Solo	Jogya- karta	Sura- baya	Malang	Medan	Palem -bang	Ujung Pandang
('000s)	8,787	3,753	795	599	292	255	1,323	291	675	407	397
	%	%	%	%	%	%	%	%	%	%	%
Market Penetration											
- sometimes take	22	25	32	11	12	27	18	16	17	26	24

Leading Brands :- Frisian Flag, Dancow

Source :- In-Search Marketing Index - 1979

Market Comment :- A growing market :- penetration in Jakarta up from 17% in 1977. The most significant recent development is the growth of the **instant** powdered milks. Young children are important in the market and adult consumption peaks in the age groups which are likely to have young children. Still a relatively up-market product.

Cough Syrup
Table 21 - Market summary by city

	Total Adults	Jakar -ta	Ban- dung	Sema- rang	Solo	Jogya- karta	Sura- baya	Malang	Medan	Palem -bang	Ujung Pandang
('000s)	8,787	3,753	795	599	292	255	1,323	291	675	407	397
	%	%	%	%	%	%	%	%	%	%	%
Market Penetration											
- sometimes take	29	30	32	16	15	20	30	18	42	24	38

Leading Brands :- Vick's Formula 44, Laserin

Source :- In-Search Marketing Index - 1979

Market comment :- In terms of sex and age the consumer profile is very similar to the population as a whole, but there is less consumption among those from lower income homes. No growth in Jakarta penetration since 1977.

Shampoo
Table 22 -Market summary by city

	Total Adults	Jakar -ta	Ban- dung	Sema- rang	Solo	Jogya- karta	Sura- baya	Malang	Medan	Palem -bang	Ujung Pandang
('000s)	8,787	3,753	795	599	292	255	1,323	291	675	407	397
	%	%	%	%	%	%	%	%	%	%	%
Market Penetration											
- sometimes use											
- Powder shampoo	57	60	64	59	53	52	59	56	47	40	59
- Liquid shampoo	35	33	38	26	31	42	41	28	36	22	45

Leading Brands :- Sunsilk, Kao, Agree, Tancho, Clinic

Source :- In-Search Marketing Index - 1979

Market Comment :- The powder sector has the advantage of lower price, and the liquid sector has a much higher income user profile. Liquid shampoo is also used disproportionately by women and younger adults.

Toothpaste
Table 23 - Market summary by city

	Total Adults	Jakar-ta	Ban-dung	Sema-rang	Solo	Jogya-karta	Sura-baya	Malang	Medan	Palem-bang	Ujung Pandang
('000s)	8,787	3,753	795	599	292	255	1,323	291	675	407	397
	%	%	%	%	%	%	%	%	%	%	%
Market Penetration											
- sometimes use	94	95	96	85	89	89	95	91	93	95	95

Leading Brands :- Pepsodent, Prodent, Signal, Colgate

Source :- In-Search Marketing Index - 1979

Market comment :- The market has been close to saturation for several years. Pepsodent is by far the dominant brand.

Butter/Margarine, Jam and Ketchup
Table 22 - Market summary by city

	Total Adults	Jakar-ta	Ban-dung	Sema-rang	Solo	Jogya-karta	Sura-baya	Malang	Medan	Palem-bang	Ujung Pandang
('000s)	8,787	3,753	795	599	292	255	1,323	291	675	407	397
	%	%	%	%	%	%	%	%	%	%	%
Market Penetration											
- sometimes take											
- Butter/Marg	45	44	54	21	25	31	43	35	43	71	87
- Ketchup	86	89	90	83	72	74	83	82	88	91	91
- Jam	18	14	22	6	7	13	22	7	29	15	49

Leading Brands :- Blue Band (Margarine), Pido, Welco (Jam),
ABC (Ketchup)

Source:- In-Search Marketing Index

Market Comment :- The butter/margarine market is growing. Festival periods are important for the margarine market because of home cake making. The ketchup market is very fragmented with many local brands operating in the regions. The Indonesian term for jam (selai) is fairly broad, encompassing bread spreads such as chocolate. Government efforts to promote the consumption of bread have been of only moderate success and rice remains very much the basic breakfast foodstuff.

Talcum Powder
Table 25 - Market summary by city

	Total Adults	Jakar -ta	Ban- dung	Sema- rang	Solo	Jogya- karta	Sura- baya	Malang	Medan	Palem -bang	Ujung Pandang
('000s)	8,787	3,753	795	599	292	255	1,323	291	675	407	397
	%	%	%	%	%	%	%	%	%	%	%
Market Penetration											
- sometimes use	18	22	16	7	8	11	15	10	18	14	29

Leading Brands :- Purol, Johnson's Baby Powder

Source :- In-Search Marketing Index - 1979

Market comment :- Purol - the clear market leader - is a **medicated** powder. Talcum powder penetration in Jakarta up from 19% in 1977. Usage is predominantly female, in the early middle age groups and among those from better-off homes.

Toilet Soap
Table 26 - Market summary by city

	Total Adults	Jakar -ta	Ban- dung	Sema- rang	Solo	Jogya- karta	Sura- baya	Malang	Medan	Palem -bang	Ujung Pandang
('000s)	8,787	3,753	795	599	292	255	1,323	291	675	407	397
	%	%	%	%	%	%	%	%	%	%	%
Market Penetration											
- sometimes use	95	94	95	91	95	96	98	95	95	95	97

Leading Brands :- Lux, Lifebuoy, Palmolive

Source :- In-Search Marketing Index - 1979

Market Comment :- A market of very high penetration with Lux the clear market leader.

Hair Cream
Table 27 - Market summary by city

	Total Adults	Jakar -ta	Ban- dung	Sema- rang	Solo	Jogya- karta	Sura- baya	Malang	Medan	Palem -bang	Ujung Pandang
('000s)	8,787	3,753	795	599	292	255	1,323	291	675	407	397
	%	%	%	%	%	%	%	%	%	%	%
Market Penetration											
- sometimes use	37	35	37	40	39	38	43	24	38	38	49

Leading Brands :- Brisk, Brylcreem

Source :- In-Search Marketing Index - 1979

Market comment :- The market is declining particularly at the younger end :- (there was a 23% decline in the number of 15-19 year olds using hair cream between 1977 and 1979). In 1979, 29% of all Jakarta users were female. Users tend to be older middle aged but this is not a particularly high income market.

Hair Conditioner
Table 28 - Market summary by city

	Total Adults	Jakar -ta	Ban- dung	Sema- rang	Solo	Jogya- karta	Sura- baya	Malang	Medan	Palem -bang	Ujung Pandang
('000s)	8,787	3,753	795	599	292	255	1,323	291	675	407	397
	%	%	%	%	%	%	%	%	%	%	%
Market Penetration											
- sometimes use	4	5	6	4	3	7	5	1	4	2	5

Leading Brands :- Sunsilk, Revlon, Wella

Source :- In-Search Marketing Index - 1979

Market Comment :- Not a large market now but expected to grow as the traditional stiff bun hair styles give way to a more natural look. Currently 71% of users are female and the market generally is young and well-off.

Perfume and Deodorant

Table 29 - Market summary by city

	Total Adults	Jakar -ta	Ban- dung	Sema- rang	Solo	Jogya- karta	Sura- baya	Malang	Medan	Palem -bang	Ujung Pandang
('000s)	8,787	3,753	795	599	292	255	1,323	291	675	407	397
	%	%	%	%	%	%	%	%	%	%	%
Market Penetration											
-sometimes use											
Aerosol deodorant	3	4	4	2	2	3	3	1	4	4	5
Stick deodorant	12	13	15	11	14	19	14	18	8	15	7
Roll-on deodorant	1	1	1	*	1	2	1	1	*	*	1
Squeeze deodorant	5	4	7	4	5	7	5	5	5	3	5
Perfume	27	27	31	12	20	25	30	15	25	23	42

Leading Brands :- Rexona (Deodorants)

Source :-   In-Search Marketing Index - 1979

Market comment :- The deodorant market has grown since 1977, with the lower priced stick deodorants dominating at present.   Perfume is included here since 43% of users are male and is probably better thought of as a deodorant.   Deodorant/perfume usage peaks in the early twenties.   Aerosol deodorant has the highest income profile of the various types.

Cosmetics

Table 30 - Market summary by city

	Total Females	Jakar -ta	Ban- dung	Sema- rang	Solo	Jogya- Karta	Sura- baya	Malang	Medan	Palem -bang	Ujung Pandang
('000s)	4,882	1,855	403	322	156	130	702	157	333	200	189
	%	%	%	%	%	%	%	%	%	%	%
Market Penetration											
- sometimes use											
- Lipstick	45	53	55	38	38	42	49	34	52	51	53
- Body lotion	13	14	20	16	11	18	14	11	13	8	15
- Face powder	63	69	73	67	67	68	75	65	70	64	62
- Face cream	20	22	31	21	17	25	21	17	22	23	22
- Hair spray	14	16	16	9	14	17	13	8	21	25	23

Leading Brands :- Viva, Revlon, Ponds, Avon (General cosmetics),Just Wonderful (Hair spray)

Source :- In-Search Marketing Index - 1979

Market Comments:- Lipstick and Body lotion are the market sectors to have shown growth since 1977. The decline in hair spray usage from 19% in Jakarta in 1977, confirms the trend towards more natural hair styles. In general these tend to be products for those from better-off homes.

Vitamin Tablets and Liquid

Table 31 - Market summary by city

	Total Adults	Jakar -ta	Ban- dung	Sema- rang	Solo	Jogya- karta	Sura- baya	Malang	Medan	Palem -bang	Ujung Pandang
('000s)	8,787	3,753	795	599	292	255	1,323	291	675	407	397
	%	%	%	%	%	%	%	%	%	%	%
Market Penetration											
- sometimes take											
- Vitamin tablets	27	24	34	13	23	29	29	17	31	28	57
- Vitamin liquid	6	8	6	3	2	4	3	2	10	7	7

Leading brands :- N.A.

Source :- In-Search Marketing Index - 1979

Market comment :- These are large markets consistent with the Indonesian health preoccupation. Women and children are relatively more important in the liquid sector. Vitamin products tend to be taken by those from middle and upper income homes although no single age group has predominant usage.

Herbal Medicine

Table 32 - Market summary by city

	Total Adults	Jakar-ta	Ban-dung	Sema-rang	Solo	Jogya-karta	Sura-baya	Malang	Medan	Palem-bang	Ujung Pandang
('000s)	8,787	3,753	795	599	292	255	1,323	291	675	407	397
	%	%	%	%	%	%	%	%	%	%	%
Market Penetration											
- sometimes take	62	63	59	60	63	69	78	74	49	50	34

Leading Brands :- Cap Jago, Nyonya Meneer, Air Mancur

Source :-   In-Search Marketing Index - 1979

Market comment :-   This is one of the largest and most interesting of Indonesia's consumer markets. Herbal remedies - Jamus - have been used for generations and the people have developed strong faith in their efficiency. Nowadays there is a wide variety of jamus to cover a great range of complaints.   Local marketing has become increasingly sophisticated with modern plant, R and D units, well planned packaging and heavy advertising. Despite being a traditional market, usage of jamus increased in Jakarta from 53% to 63% between 1977 and 1979.

Beer and Stout

Table 33 - Market summary by city

	Total Adults	Jakar -ta	Ban- dung	Sema- rang	Solo	Jogya- karta	Sura- baya	Malang	Medan	Palem -bang	Ujung Pandang
('000s)	8,787	3,753	795	599	292	255	1,323	291	675	407	397
	%	%	%	%	%	%	%	%	%	%	%
Market Penetration											
- sometimes take											
- Beer	14	13	13	10	8	8	15	9	24	17	18
- Stout	5	5	4	1	1	1	4	2	16	5	11

Leading Brands :- Bintang, Anchor (Beer), Guinness (Stout)

Source :- In-Search Marketing Index - 1979

Market comment :- The predominant Islamic religion will always be a constraining factor on the alcoholic beverage markets of Indonesia. However, the Faith is not as strictly adhered to as on the neighbouring Malay Peninsula and beer/stout has become a sizeable minority market. Beer tends to be a social, out of home drink while Guinness tends to be consumed in home for recuperative/tonic reasons (and has some sexual overtones for men). The higher incidence of alcohol consumption in Medan may be partly explained by its disproportionate Chinese population, and the relatively high proportion of Christian Bataks who also drink.

Soft Drinks

Table 34 - Market summary by city

	Total Adults	Jakar -ta	Ban- dung	Sema- rang	Solo	Jogya- karta	Sura- baya	Malang	Medan	Palem -bang	Ujung Pandang
('000s)	8,787	3,753	795	599	292	255	1,323	291	675	407	397
	%	%	%	%	%	%	%	%	%	%	%
Market Penetration											
- sometimes take	59	65	70	32	35	44	55	31	70	65	50

Leading Brands :-   Sosro Tea Botol, Fanta (red), Green Spot, Sprite,
Coca Cola

Source :- In-Search Marketing Index - 1979

Market Comment :- The leading brand is a sweet cold bottled tea which
has grown considerably in recent years and benefits from the
traditional appeal of tea as a drink and a low price. The general view
is that carbonated drinks are 'stronger' and not so suitable for
children. From this point of view the carbonated colas are at something of a disadvantage.

Confectionery and Ice Cream
Table 35 - Market summary by city

	Total Adults	Jakar -ta	Ban- dung	Sema- rang	Solo	Jogya- karta	Sura- baya	Malang	Medan	Palem -bang	Ujung Pandang
('000s)	8,787	3,753	795	599	292	255	1,323	291	675	407	397
	%	%	%	%	%	%	%	%	%	%	%
Market Penetration											
- sometimes take											
- Chewing gum	14	12	19	7	8	12	15	5	22	15	23
- Ice Cream	25	22	32	11	12	21	28	10	50	18	39
- Chocolate	19	16	34	13	10	18	24	11	22	14	23
- Medicated Sweets	14	13	19	9	11	14	23	8	12	11	13
- Sugar confectionery	38	34	49	29	24	16	41	34	50	43	37

Leading brands :- Chicklets (Chewing gum), Sugus, Halls,
Flipper, Woody (Ice cream)

Source :- In-Search Marketing Index - 1979

Market comment :- Not much growth in this market at present. Ice cream and chocolate are consumed more by women, chewing gum and medicated sweets more by men. Chewing gum has declined from 18% penetration in Jakarta in 1977.

Razor Blades and After-Shave

Table 36 - Market summary by city

	Total Males	Jakar -ta	Ban- dung	Sema- rang	Solo	Jogya- karta	Sura- baya	Malang	Medan	Palem -bang	Ujung Pandang
('000s)	3,904	1,895	390	279	136	125	623	133	344	207	208
	%	%	%	%	%	%	%	%	%	%	%
Market Penetration											
- sometimes use											
- Razor blades	74	65	70	53	65	66	70	65	62	76	79
- After Shave	4	5	5	1	2	2	2	2	2	1	4

Leading brands :- Goal, Tiger, Nacet (Blades), Old Spice, Tabac, Mandom (After shave).

Source :- In-Search Marketing Index - 1979

Market comment :- In addition to the men shown above, 31% of women in Jakarta also claim to use razor blades. After shave is predominantly an up-market product.

Worm Medicine

Table 37 - Market summary by city

	Total Adults	Jakar -ta	Ban- dung	Sema- rang	Solo	Jogya- karta	Sura- haya	Malang	Medan	Palem -bang	Ujung Pandang
('000s)	8,787	3,753	795	599	292	255	1,323	291	675	407	397
	%	%	%	%	%	%	%	%	%	%	%
Market Penetration											
- sometimes take	9	11	4	3	3	5	1	2	21	10	22

Leading Brands :- Upixon, Combantrin

Source :- In-Search Marketing Index - 1979

Market Comment :- There are twice as many female as male users and usage tends to be with the middle-aged. The market profile is not particularly low income.

Plaster for Cuts

Table 38 - Market summary by city

	Total Adults	Jakar -ta	Ban- dung	Sema- rang	Solo	Jogya- karta	Sura- baya	Malang	Medan	Palem -bang	Ujung Pandang
('000s)	8,787	3,753	795	599	292	255	1,323	291	675	407	397
	%	%	%	%	%	%	%	%	%	%	%
Market Penetration											
- sometimes buy	43	43	55	34	36	44	35	34	55	51	54

Leading Brands :- Band-aid, Tensoplast, Handyplast

Source :- In-Search Marketing Index - 1979

Market comment :- A growing market with Jakarta penetration up from 30% in 1977. There is no strong socio-economic bias to the market but users tend to be the younger adults.

Ball Pens

Table 39 - Market summary by city

	Total Adults	Jakar -ta	Ban- dung	Sema- rang	Solo	Jogya- karta	Sura- baya	Malang	Medan	Palem -bang	Ujung Pandang
('000s)	8,787	3,753	795	599	292	255	1,323	291	675	407	397
	%	%	%	%	%	%	%	%	%	%	%
Market Penetration											
- sometimes buy	39	37	53	36	39	47	35	34	46	38	45

Leading Brands :- Bic, Pilot

Source :- In-Search Marketing Index - 1979

Market Comment :- This is a market in which usage has increased since 1977 (in Jakarta up from 47% to 55% of adults) but not the incidence of purchasing. This is consistent with an improvement in literacy levels. 1979 purchasing is predominantly male and by younger adults. (It would not be unusual to see just a refill wrapped with paper or tape being used).

Insecticide

Table 40 - Market summary by city

	Total Adults	Jakar -ta	Ban- dung	Sema- rang	Solo	Jogya- karta	Sura- baya	Malang	Medan	Palem -bang	Ujung Pandang
('000s)	8,787	3,753	795	599	292	255	1,323	291	675	407	397
	%	%	%	%	%	%	%	%	%	%	%
Market Penetration											
- sometimes buy											
Liquid insecticide	18	22	9	12	9	7	20	4	18	16	14
Aerosol insecticide	5	4	11	2	3	8	5	6	6	3	5
Mosquito coils	41	37	44	42	46	44	32	31	48	63	58

Leading Brands :- Baygon, Raid, Mortein (Aerosol/Liquid)

Source :- In-Search Marketing Index - 1979

Market comment :- Since 1977 Liquid insecticide has grown in purchase incidence while aerosol insecticide and mosquito coils have not. The lower price of liquid insecticides is an important factor in its market strength. The aerosol profile is relatively up-market by comparison with liquid.

Air Freshener

Table 41 - Market summary by city

	Total Adults	Jakar -ta	Ban- dung	Sema- rang	Solo	Jogya- Karta	Sura- baya	Malang	Medan	Palem -bang	Ujung Pandang
('000s)	8,787	3,753	795	599	292	255	1,323	291	675	407	397
	%	%	%	%	%	%	%	%	%	%	%
Market Penetration											
- sometimes buy	2	2	6	1	1	2	2	1	3	1	2

Leading Brands :- Glade, Bayfresh

Source :- In-Search Marketing Index - 1979

Market Comment :- Essentially a female purchase in a high income market.

Floor Cleaner
Table 42 - Market summary by city

	Total Adults	Jakar-ta	Ban-dung	Sema-rang	Solo	Jogya-karta	Sura-baya	Malang	Medan	Palem-bang	Ujung Pandang
('000s)	8,787	3,753	795	599	292	255	1,323	291	675	407	397
	%	%	%	%	%	%	%	%	%	%	%
Market Penetration											
- sometimes buy	8	8	15	6	7	9	9	6	6	4	3

Leading brands :- Densol, Axi

Source :- In-Search Marketing Index - 1979

Market comment :- Another market in which purchasing is predominantly by women. Although not extreme, it is a relatively up-market product.

Batteries
Table 43 - Market summary by city

	Total Adults	Jakar-ta	Ban-dung	Sema-rang	Solo	Jogya-karta	Sura-baya	Malang	Medan	Palem-bang	Ujung Pandang
('000s)	8,787	3,753	795	599	292	255	1,323	291	675	407	397
	%	%	%	%	%	%	%	%	%	%	%
Market Penetration											
- sometimes buy	35	31	43	39	33	41	33	29	38	39	39

Leading Brands :- Ever-Ready, A.B.C.

Source :- In-Search Marketing Index - 1979

Market Comment :- There has been a fall in the incidence of battery purchasing since 1977 (Jakarta down from 46% and Surabaya from 49%). The purchaser profile is closely in line with the population as a whole.

Bar Soap and Detergent
Table 44 - Market summary by city

	Total Adults	Jakar -ta	Ban- dung	Sema- rang	Solo	Jogya- karta	Sura- baya	Malang	Medan	Palem -bang	Ujung Pandang
('000s)	8,787	3,753	795	599	292	255	1,323	291	675	407	397
	%	%	%	%	%	%	%	%	%	%	%
Market Penetration											
- sometimes buy											
- Bar soap	15	7	11	9	3	8	8	19	47	63	34
- Cream detergent	43	47	52	47	42	43	42	47	23	5	53
- Powder detergent	27	24	33	21	21	27	25	19	36	52	29

Leading brands :- B.29, Sunlight (Bar), B-29, Rinso, Dino, Wing (Cream/powder)

Source :-   In-Search Marketing Index - 1979

Market comment :-   Not much change in market penetration since 1977. Powder detergent has a somewhat higher income profile than the other products.   More than 70% of purchasers are women.

Seasoning Powder
Table 45 - Market summary by city

	Total Adults	Jakar -ta	Ban- dung	Sema- rang	Solo	Jogya- karta	Sura- baya	Malang	Medan	Palem -bang	Ujung Pandang
('000s)	8,787	3,753	795	599	292	255	1,323	291	675	407	397
	%	%	%	%	%	%	%	%	%	%	%
Market Penetration											
- sometimes buy	42	43	48	42	39	40	37	42	36	49	48

Leading Brands :-   Aji-No-Moto, Sasa, Miwon

Source :-   In-Search Marketing Index - 1979

Market Comment :-   A market in which very small unit purchases prevail. It is possible to buy single packs for 2 Rupiah (currently about one seventh of an English penny).   A large market whose profile closely resembles the population as a whole.

Cooking Oil

Table 46 - Market summary by city

	Total Adults	Jakar -ta	Ban- dung	Sema- rang	Solo	Jogya- karta	Sura- baya	Malang	Medan	Palem -bang	Ujung Pandang
('000s)	8,787	3,753	795	599	292	255	1,323	291	675	407	397
	%	%	%	%	%	%	%	%	%	%	%
Market Penetration											
- sometimes buy	43	44	48	42	39	39	38	43	44	52	42

Leading brands :- Barco, Delfia, Sintanola

Source :- In-Search Marketing Index - 1979

Market comment :- No growth in Jakarta penetration since 1977. Predominantly a female purchase with no socio-economic market bias.

Cigarettes

Table 47 - Market summary by city

	Total Adults	Jakar -ta	Ban- dung	Sema- rang	Solo	Jogya- karta	Sura- baya	Malang	Medan	Palem -bang	Ujung Pandang
('000s)	8,787	3,753	795	599	292	255	1,323	291	675	407	397
	%	%	%	%	%	%	%	%	%	%	%
Smoke cigarettes											
regularly	28	30	29	25	24	27	22	24	34	31	29

Leading Brands :- Gudang Garam, Bentoel, Menak Jinggo, Jarum Coklat (Kretek), Commodore, Gold Bond, Mascot, Indo Jaya (White)

Source :- In-Search Marketing Index - 1979

Market Comment :- In overall terms the market is dominated by a type of cigarette known as **Kretek** which is made from a mixture of tobacco and spices, and herbs (cloves). It is a high tar/high nicotine cigarette but believed to be a 'cooling' smoke. Kretek cigarettes comprise approximately three quarters of the total market. The exception is the island of Sumatra where the more conventional **white** cigarettes predominate.

Sanitary Protection
Table 48 - Market summary by city

	Total Females	Jakar -ta	Ban- dung	Sema- rang	Solo	Jogya- Karta	Sura- baya	Malang	Medan	Palem -bang	Ujung Pandang
('000s)	4,882	1,855	403	322	156	130	702	157	333	200	189
Market Penetration %	%	%	%	%	%	%	%	%	%	%	%
- sometimes use	28	33	28	21	28	30	38	24	30	23	26

Leading brands :- Intex, Softex, Stayfree

Source :- In-Search Marketing Index - 1979

Market comment :- In Jakarta the market peaks with the 20-24 year olds of whom 44% use a sanitary protection product - and declines with age to 24% of the 35-39's and 12% of the 40-49's.   The market is growing (1977 penetration in Jakarta was 20%) and disproportionately for the beltless napkins.   The alternative to a branded sanitary protection product is are re-usable piece of towelling known as a 'Duk'.

Tonic Wine
Table 49 - Market summary by city

	Total Adults	Jakar -ta	Ban- dung	Sema- rang	Solo	Jogya- karta	Sura- baya	Malang	Medan	Palem -bang	Ujung Pandang
('000s)	8,787	5,753	795	599	292	255	1,323	291	675	407	397
	%	%	%	%	%	%	%	%	%	%	%
Market Penetration											
- sometimes take	13	9	13	8	12	16	20	9	15	19	18

Leading Brands :- Tonikum Bayer, Durol.

Source :- In-Search Marketing Index - 1979

Market Comment :- Jakarta market penetration down from 17% in 1977. Consumption is predominantly male and tends to be found in the middle age group and the middle-upper end of the socio-economic scale.

4 Consumer markets — durable and other

As with the previous section the objective here is to provide summary information for the major durable and other markets for 10 major conurbations.

It should be noted that ownership of household appliances is based on a sample of people and market sizes are in terms of the proportions of all adults living in homes with each appliance. However, because of the way the sampling was carried out for the survey concerned the percentages given should approximate to within a few per cent of the 'proportion of households owning'.

Many of the consumer durable markets are constrained by the absence of electricity in the home. Even where a power supply exists the available wattage may well be limited. This entails additional cost to increase it for new appliances.

Not surprisingly, the consumer durable markets do tend to be upper income in profile although there are signs of growth down the socio-economic scale.

Despite a certain amount of anti Japanese feeling which showed itself in the anti-Tanaka riots, the Japanese have been the most significant investors in the durable markets and today supply many of the leading brands. The Japanese are now extremely well placed for any consumer durable take-off which may occur in the next decade.

It will be seen that variations in consumer durable ownership are quite large across the ten cities reflecting the enormous variety of household background that exists in Indonesia.

Television and Radio
Table 50 - Market summary by city

	Total Adults	Jakar -ta	Ban- dung	Sema- rang	Solo	Jogya- karta	Sura- baya	Malang	Medan	Palem -bang	Ujung Pandang
('000s)	8,787	3,753	795	599	292	255	1,323	291	675	407	397
Live in household with	%	%	%	%	%	%	%	%	%	%	%
Television	50	53	54	36	37	44	55	37	51	46	39
Radio	70	69	76	66	75	83	71	66	68	63	61

Source :- In-Search Marketing Index - 1979

Market comment :- Television ownership is increasing :- the incidence of adults in a TV home in Jakarta was 38% in 1977. Colour TV penetration was low in 1980 (e.g. 5% of homes in Jakarta). Electricity is a limiting factor for TV ownership :- In 1979 only 44% of adults lived in a home with electricity. Where no electricity exists, car batteries are used and re-charge facilities are readily available. Radio ownership has not grown since 1977.

Gas Cooker and Refrigerator
Table 51 - Market summary by city

	Total Adults	Jakar -ta	Ban- dung	Sema- rang	Solo	Jogya- karta	Sura- baya	Malang	Medan	Palem -bang	Ujung Pandang
('000s)	8,787	3,753	795	599	292	255	1,323	291	675	407	397
Live in household with	%	%	%	%	%	%	%	%	%	%	%
- Gas cooker	5	5	6	3	2	2	5	1	5	4	3
- Refrigerator	15	17	15	7	9	7	19	7	13	12	12

Source :- In-Search Marketing Index - 1979

Market comment :- Both markets have grown since 1977. In Jakarta in 1977 4% lived in a home with a gas cooker and 10% had a refrigerator. Not surprisingly these are both higher income markets. The most common forms of cooking in Indonesia are by kerosene stove (mainly) or charcoal/wood.

Motor Cycles
Table 52 - Market summary by city

	Total Adults	Jakar -ta	Ban- dung	Sema- rang	Solo	Jogya- karta	Sura- baya	Malang	Medan	Palem -bang	Ujung Pandang
('000s)	8,787	3,753	795	599	292	255	1,323	291	675	407	397
Live in household with	%	%	%	%	%	%	%	%	%	%	%
- Motorcycle	26	21	30	24	26	34	37	20	34	13	34

Source :-   In-Search Marketing Index - 1979

Market comment :-   The market has been growing since 1977, but remains disproportionately upper income.   There is considerable variation in the performance of makes across the country.   For example, Honda leads in Jakarta, Medan, Bandang, Jogyakarta and Malang; Yamaha leads in Surabaya, Solo and Ujung Pandang; Vespa leads in Palembang and Semarang

Motor Cars
Table 53 - Market summary by city

	Total Adults	Jakar -ta	Ban- dung	Sema- rang	Solo	Jogya- karta	Sura- baya	Malang	Medan	Palem -bang	Ujung Pandang
('000s)	8,787	3,753	795	599	292	255	1,323	291	675	407	397
	%	%	%	%	%	%	%	%	%	%	%
Live in household with - Motor car	6	7	8	4	4	4	5	4	5	4	3

Source :-   In-Search Marketing Index - 1979

Market comment :-   No growth in market penetration since 1977, and very much a high income ownership.   The market has a strong Japanese presence through Datsun, Toyota, Mazda and Honda with Peugeot and Fiat the strongest of the European makes.

Other Electric Appliances
Table 54 - Market summary by city

	Total Adults	Jakar -ta	Ban- dung	Sema- rang	Solo	Jogya- karta	Sura- baya	Malang	Medan	Palem -bang	Ujung Pandang
('000s)	8,787	3,753	795	599	292	255	1,323	291	675	407	397
Live in household with	%	%	%	%	%	%	%	%	%	%	%
- Sewing machine	53	52	53	40	46	47	58	38	67	58	58
- Electric iron	31	31	40	17	20	23	43	22	22	31	35
- Air conditioner	1	1	*	*	*	*	1		*	*	1
- Tape recorder	25	21	28	24	24	29	38	27	26	27	11
- Fan	17	19	6	11	10	8	29	4	20	20	14

Source :- In-Search Marketing Index - 1979

Market comment :- Of these markets the only significant growth in penetration since 1977 has been for electric irons. Sewing machines have very strong penetration for a consumer durable in a country of low average income. They are sought after in both the rural and urban areas and are used to both save and earn money. Singer is the dominant brand

Cameras
Table 55 - Market summary by city

	Total Adults	Jakar -ta	Ban- dung	Sema- rang	Solo	Jogya- karta	Sura- baya	Malang	Medan	Palem -bang	Ujung Pandang
('000s)	8,787	3,753	795	599	292	255	1,323	291	675	407	397
	%	%	%	%	%	%	%	%	%	%	%
Live in household with											
- Camera	11	13	11	7	9	12	12	7	12	6	6

Source :- In-Search Marketing Index - 1979

Market comment :- The market has grown since 1977, particularly in Jakarta when 8% of adults lived in a home with a camera. As with the other consumer durables this is an upper-income product. Canon and Fujica lead the market.

Wrist Watches

Table 56 - Market summary by city

	Total Adults	Jakar-ta	Ban-dung	Sema-rang	Solo	Jogya-karta	Sura-baya	Malang	Medan	Palem-bang	Ujung Pandang
('000s)	8,787	3,753	795	599	292	255	1,323	291	675	407	397
	%	%	%	%	%	%	%	%	%	%	%
Market penetration											
own a wrist watch	N.A.	36	42	N.A.	N.A.	41	37	N.A.	38	32	N.A.

Source :- In-Search Marketing Index - 1979

Market comment :- Higher ownership among men than women (e.g. 44% of men in Jakarta owned a watch). Seiko is the clear market leader :- other leading brands are Citizen, Garuda and Titus: as expected, the market has a higher income socio-economic bias.

5 Tourist markets

THE POTENTIAL OF TOURISM

As with many other markets in Indonesia, tourism is an area of potential which is only just beginning to be realised now. In 1979 there were 493,000 foreign visitors :- an increase of 282% over 1970, but still well behind neighbouring Singapore's figure which was in excess of two million foreign visitors for the same year.

The Government has recognised the potential of tourism and is planning to attract one million foreign tourists by the end of Repelita III. Tourism would then be the nation's fourth largest source of foreign exchange earnings.

In 1980 25 international airlines were flying into Indonesia. The main gateways are Jakarta, Bali and Medan and three more are soon to be added - Menado in Sulawesi, Padang in West Sumatra and Biak in Irian Jaya. Priority is being given to investment in hotel development and there are plans for developing more regional tourist centres.

In the short term, growth in tourism is unlikely to be dramatic. Promotional budgets are still on the low side (about one sixth of Singapore's in 1978/1979) and competition from within the Region is stiff. Obtaining visas can be difficult for foreigners and the whole infrastructure of roads and airports is insufficiently developed.

By comparison with its Asian neighbours, Indonesia tends to be a destination for long haul tourists from Europe, Japan and America and these visitors are more vulnerable to world wide economic pressures than regional travellers.

Nevertheless Indonesia has many areas of natural beauty, rich and diverse cultures. With Government's recognition of tourism's potential and action in hand, the medium term prognosis looks sound.

CURRENT MARKET PROFILE

The main source of information on tourism is the Directorate General of Tourism which provides analyses of immigration statistics. Jakarta and Bali are the main points of entry to Indonesia and in 1979 accounted for 85% of foreign visitor arrivals. Bali has been growing as a visitor entry point and through the Seventies its share increased from 18% to 27% of visitor arrivals.

Table 57 - Number and distribution of foreign visitor arrivals by major port of entry

	Total Visitors ('000s)		Major port of entry(%)			
			Jakarta	Bali	Medan	Others
1970	129	%	59.9	17.8	7.8	14.5
1971	179	%	60.5	18.1	8.3	13.1
1972	221	%	60.1	21.4	8.0	10.5
1973	270	%	63.3	19.9	8.8	8.0
1974	313	%	64.0	17.1	9.1	9.8
1975	366	%	58.3	20.6	9.0	12.1
1976	451	%	50.4	25.5	11.0	12.9
1977	487	%	46.6	24.5	13.5	15.5
1978	467	%	54.6	28.5	8.4	8.5
1979	493	%	58.3	26.7	9.6	5.4

Source :- Directorate General of Tourism

Australia, Japan, U.S.A. and Singapore are the countries from which most tourists originate although the visitor profile varies considerably depending on the point of entry. Australians, for example, made up almost a third of all visitor arrivals to Bali but only 6.2% of arrivals to Jakarta. Visitors from Singapore accounted for almost 16% in Jakarta but only 1.4% of Bali arrivals. In short, visitors from the region are more likely to arrive at Jakarta.

Table 58 - Country of residence profile of foreign visitors

| | Port of entry | |
	Jakarta (1979)	Bali (1978)
	%	%
Country of residence		
- USA	9.6	13.3
- Canada	1.3	2.1
- France	6.3	4.5
- Germany	5.8	5.5
- Italy	2.3	4.6
- Switzerland	1.7	2.3
- England	4.0	4.2
- Benelux	11.1	1.6
- Australia	6.2	31.3
- New Zealand	0.8	2.0
- Malaysia	6.8	0.3
- Philippines	1.6	0.1
- Singapore	15.9	1.4
- Thailand	2.4	0.3
- Hong Kong	1.9	0.8
- India	1.3	0.1
- Japan	11.2	17.8
- Taiwan	3.2	0.6
- Others	6.9	7.0

Source :- Directorate General of Immigration

The tendency for regional visitors to arrive at Jakarta ties in with a tendency for the Jakarta arrivals to be visiting on business. Almost 30% of Jakarta arrivals had some business reason for the visit compared with only 6% of Bali arrivals.

Table 59 - Foreign visitors' purpose of visit

	Port of entry	
	Jakarta (1979)	Bali (1978)
	%	%
Purpose of Visit		
- Holiday	61.3	91.6
- Business	21.3	3.1
- Business and pleasure	8.6	2.8
- Other	8.8	2.5

Source :- Directorate General of Tourism

Visitors to Indonesia appear to stay for relatively long periods by comparison with the rest of the region. About half of all visitors stay in the country for fifteen days or more. In excess of 80% stay in hotels - most of the remainder stay with friends/relatives.

One implication of the long average stay is that Indonesia may be missing out in its share of those package holidays which include just a few days in a selection of countries. As a comparison, the average length of visitor stay in nearby Singapore was only 3.7 days in 1979.

**Table 60 - Foreign visitors' duration of stay
and accommodation**

| | Port of entry | |
	Jakarta (1979)	Bali (1978)
	%	%
Duration of stay		
- Less than 24 hours	0.1	
1-3 days	1.2	1.3
4-7 days	7.9	16.4
8-14 days	37.2	33.5
15+ days	53.6	48.8
Accommodation		
- Hotels	81.0	84.4
- Other	19.0	15.6

Source :- Directorate General of Immigration

Information from the Jakarta immigration office shows that in 1979 July was the peak month for foreign visitors with 30,837. January to May is the time of fewest arrivals with figures at around two thirds of the July figure each month.

Official statistics put the 1978 total number of hotels at 3,120 - an increase of 4.5% over the previous year - which offered in excess of 50,000 beds. Average hotel occupancy rates were estimated in 1979 at around 50% for both Jakarta and Bali.

Table 61 - Hotels, rooms and beds available

	Hotels/ Lodging Houses	Rooms	Beds
Total	3,120	57,160	104,426
Sumatra	680	10,600	20,463
Java	1,618	33,179	59,755
Bali and Nusa Tenggara	293	5,563	10,567
Kalimantan	271	4,314	7,358
Sulawesi	212	2,928	5,181
Maluku and Irian Jaya	46	576	1,102

Source :- Indonesian Annual Statistics (1978)

Statistics from the city of Jakarta show a 1979 hotel profile of 2% (5 Star), 6% (4 Star), 7% (3 Star), 15% (2 Star), 7% (1 Star) and 63% (No Star). It should be added that the No Star category only accounted for 29% of available rooms whereas 3-Star to 5-Star hotels accounted for 52% of rooms.

Demographic information for Jakarta foreign visitors shows that in 1979, 72% were male, again consistent with the higher business orientation for the capital.

Estimates of foreign tourist expenditure are as follows:-

Table 62 - Foreign visitor expenditure (US$ million)

Expenditure category	1974	1978
- Accommodation	15	N.A.
- Food and beverage	10	N.A.
- Local transport and entertainment	6	N.A.
- Souvenirs	8	N.A.
- Other	4	N.A.
Total	43	98

Source :- Directorate General of Tourism

There is a limited amount of information available on overseas travel by Indonesian citizens. The following figures show the growing numbers of citizens departing through Jakarta in the latter part of the Seventies.The figures will include sizeable numbers of Moslem pilgrims.

Table 63 - Indonesian citizens travelling outside Indonesia via Jakarta by year

	1975	1976	1977	1978	1979
Departures ('000s)					
- By air	171	170	223	289	242
- By sea	3	2	1	*	*
- Total	173	172	224	289	242

Source :- Jakarta Office of Immigration

6 Financial markets

STRUCTURE

Indonesia's financial system essentially consists of the following institutions :-

- Bank Indonesia
- 93 commercial banks
- 28 development banks
- Other financial institutions

BANK INDONESIA

Bank Indonesia fulfils most of those functions normally carried out by a central bank, and exerts a strong influence on the financial system:

- It regulates money supply, credit policy and interest rates.
- It regulates the liquidity position of banks and minimum reserve requirements.
- It advises the Government on monetary policy, it holds the treasury accounts and makes necessary advances to the Government.
- It is the sole issuer of Indonesian currency and holds the official international reserves.
- It regulates all financial institutions except insurance companies.
- It provides substantial rediscount and refinancing facilities.

STATE OWNED COMMERCIAL BANKS

There are five State owned commercial banks which dominate commercial banking. At March 1979 they accounted for 83% of total outstanding bank credits. Each bank provides services to a specific sector of the economy.

> Bank Rakyat Indonesia - Smallholder agricultural and
>   rural development
>
> Bank Bumi Daya   - estate agriculture and forestry
>
> Bank Negara Indonesia - industry and industrial
>   infrastructure
>
> Bank Dagang Negara   - mining
>
> Bank Ekspor - Impor Indonesia - export, import
> financing

These banks are funded in about equal proportion by demand and time deposits - the latter to a maximum of 24 months. They are also the major beneficiaries of Bank Indonesia refinancing schemes of which the largest is for credit to rice farmers for fertilizer and other agricultural aids.

NATIONAL PRIVATE BANKS

In 1980 there were 77 national private banks with activities similar to those of the State banks. This sector has been encouraged by Government with liquidity support and tax incentives for merging to improve efficiency and working capital. Only 9 of these banks are licensed to engage in foreign exchange transactions.

At March 1979 the national private banks accounted for 9% of total outstanding credits.

FOREIGN BANKS

At mid 1980 there were 10 foreign banks in Jakarta (each is allowed a maximum of two branches in Jakarta and more elsewhere). These were :-

> American Express International Banking Corp.
> Citibank N.A.
> The Chase Manhatten Bank N.A.
> Bangkok Bank Ltd.
> Bank of America National Trust and Saving Assoc.
> The Chartered Bank
> The Hong Kong and Shanghai Banking Corp.
> The Bank of Tokyo Ltd.
> European Asian Bank A.G.
> Algemene Bank Nederland N.V.

In addition there is one joint venture with a local Indonesian group - PT Bank Perdania - and 50 representative offices of foreign banks not directly engaged in domestic banking.

In line with Bank Indonesia's policy of encouraging national private banks, no new foreign banks have been granted permits since 1970.

At March 1979 the foreign banks accounted for 8% of total outstanding credits.

DEVELOPMENT BANKS

In 1980 there were 28 development banks consisting of 26 regional banks wholly or partly owned by provincial governments, one privately owned and one State bank. The State bank - The Development Bank of Indonesia - is the largest and has been authorised to grant 15 year loans (although most credits are for 5 years).

In addition to the development banks there are three development finance institutions which provide an additional source of long term financing but are not authorized to accept deposits from the public. They are joint ventures between Indonesian banks and enterprises and foreign banks.

INVESTMENT FINANCE COMPANIES

There were nine investment finance companies in 1980 with similar functions to the development finance companies but are not allowed to make direct loans. Their role is more that of a money and capital market institution than that of a long term finance company. Eight of the nine companies are joint ventures between Indonesian State and private commercial banks and foreign banks.

OTHER FINANCIAL INSTITUTIONS

P.T. Papan Sejahtera was established in March 1980 as a joint venture company (local and foreign) whose main function is to provide medium and long term loans for lower class house ownership. It also gathers funds by issuing medium and long term housing bonds and taking special deposits from those wishing to purchase houses.

P.T. Danareksa was established in 1976 to help in the development of the securities market by encouraging the spread of share ownership. It may take up to 50% of any new issue for division into smaller denominations and sale through banks and other authorized outlets. A future aim is to develop a unit trust.

The Jakarta Stock Exchange had its first listing in 1977. There are incentives in terms of tax relief for companies willing to sell shares on the exchange and for investors who are prepared to buy the shares.

Table 64 - Consolidated balance sheet of the monetary system at end of 1978 and 1979 (Rp billions)

	1978	1979
Total assets/liabilities	**5.749**	**7,784**
Net foreign assets	1,704	3,483
Public sector claims		
- Central Govt.	- 878	-1,750
- Claims on official entities and public enterprises	2,796	3,282
- Govt. blocked account	- 476	- 391
Private sector claims		
- Loans	2,494	2,993
- Other	111	167
Import deposits	174	213
Currency	1,240	1,545
Demand deposits	1,248	1,771
Quasi money	1,320	1,843
Other	1,767	2,412

Source :- Bank Indonesia

Table 65 - Consolidated balance sheet of deposit money banks at end 1979 (Rp billion)

	1979
Total assets/liabilities	**6,832**
Reserves	804
Foreign assets	1,316
Public sector claims	
- Central Govt.	53
- Official entities and public enterprises	1,193
Private sector claims	
- Loans	2,973
- Other	142
Other assets	351
Demand deposits	1,674
Time/savings deposits	1,146
Foreign currency deposits	670
Foreign liabilities	431
Govt. deposits	412
Import deposits	213
Borrowings from Bank Indonesia	1,238
Capital accounts	501
Other liabilities	546

Source :- Bank Indonesia

EXCHANGE RATE

Under the Central Banking Act of 1968, Bank Indonesia is responsible for the stability of the Rupiah. From August 1971 until November 1978 the exchange rate was fixed at Rp415 per U.S.Dollar. On November 15th 1978 the Rp was devalued by 33.6% and since then has been adjusted daily according to a basket of other currencies. The middle exchange rate has stayed within Rp621 to Rp629 per U.S.Dollar.

MONEY SUPPLY

Money supply (currency plus demand deposits) grew by 35.8% in 1979 compared with 24.0% the year before. This is seen as a function of the growing need for finance in the business sector and the growth in foreign exchange earnings resulting in the rise in prices of Indonesia's commodities.

Table 66 - Money Supply (Rp billion)

	1977	(% Annual change)	1978	(% Annual change)	1979	(% Annual change)
Money supply M1	2,006	(25.1)	2,488	(24.0)	3,379	(35.8)
- Currency in circulation	979	(25.4)	1,240	(26.7)	1,545	(24.6)
- Demand deposits	1,027	(24.9)	1,248	(21.5)	1,833	(46.9)
Quasi money	1,125	(9.4)	1,320	(17.3)	1,843	(39.6)

Source :- Bank Indonesia

7 Industrial markets

MANUFACTURING

Indonesia's third 5 year development plan - Repelita III (to fiscal year 1983/84) - emphasizes the development of industries producing manufactured goods. Annual growth in the manufacturing sector for Repelita III has been projected at 11% per annum. The target is for the manufacturing industry to take 12% of GNP at the end of Repelita III compared with an actual 10% at the outset (i.e.to FY 1978/79).

It is not an easy matter to obtain an up to date statistical picture of Indonesia's manufacturing sector. There is the Annual Survey of Large and Medium Manufacturing Establishments (i.e. those employing 20 or more persons) and at the time of going to press 1978 information was available. However, given Indonesia's 'loose' system of paying tax there are some doubts about the accuracy of company returns. However, Tables 69 and 70 are taken from this survey and give at least an indication of the size and value added of some of the major industrial activities (i.e. apart from those directly concerned with Indonesia's principal primary products).

Whatever the reliability of gross output and value added figures the quarterly index of manufacturing production is a good indication of relative growth rates for some of the more important industry groups. Since 1975 there has been disproportionately high growth in the following industries :- cement, fertilizer, plywood, iron and steel products, milk products, tyres and tubes.

Table 67 – Quarterly index of manufacturing production for selected industry groups (Quarterly average 1975 = 100)

	Quarterly average 1978	Q.1.	Q.2.	Q.3.	Q.4.
			1979		
Milk, butter, cream products	173	182	199	230	192
Malt and malt liquors	105	95	104	110	124
Clove cigarettes	122	117	115	124	120
White cigarettes	116	125	119	126	152
Yarn and thread	112	106	111	106	117
Weaving mills products	112	123	126	119	118
Batik	117	113	132	114	110
Knitting mills products	90	82	76	73	-
Footwear	119	102	106	106	107
Plywood	218	174	195	257	254
Paper	134	140	150	148	140
Chemicals except fertilizer	87	94	94	138	-
Fertilizer	192	224	264	376	312
Paint, varnish, lacquer	101	93	94	107	98
Matches	124	124	139	142	135
Tyres and tubes	203	211	236	227	236
Glass products	160	137	152	166	-
Cement	255	302	316	303	318
Basic iron and steel products	180	164	265	607	-
Structural metal products	154	146	151	162	162
Dry cell batteries	165	127	184	191	219
TV, radio, video equipment	232	191	226	232	-
Motor vehicles	136	80	126	119	-
Motor cycles	89	51	81	81	-
General Index	146	140	150	164	-

Source :- Central Bureau of Statistics

The development of Indonesia's manufacturing industry is largely under the control of the Investment Co-ordinating Board (BKPM). A main contribution since its inception in 1977 has been to reduce bureaucratic delay in processing investment applications.

Approved investment areas are defined in line with the individual objectives of Repelita III. Each year BKPM publishes "List of Priority Scales for Fields of Foreign Investment for the Year 1980", a list of investment areas open to foreigners together with conditions and incentives. The closed sections tend to be those with low technological requirements and low capital needs. The open categories are many and diverse. Some of the top priority manufacturing categories for 1980 were :-

tobacco products	structural clay products
garments	cement, lime, plaster
wood working industries	other non-metallic mineral products
pulp, paper, board	basic iron, steel production
basic industrial chemicals	non-ferrous basic metal
pesticides	fabricated metal products
synthetic resin and plastic materials	engines and turbines
raw materials for drugs and medicine	machinery and equipment
other chemical products	electrical machinery and apparatus
rubber products	communications equipment
pottery, china, earthware	electrical appliances
glass, glass products	transport equipment
	professional and scientific equipment

The manufacturing sector accounted for two-thirds of domestic and foreign approved investment project finance at March 1980.

Table 68 - Distribution of foreign and domestic investment in
approved projects by economic activity (1967-1980 March)

	Approved foreign investment projects (US$8,437.2 million)	Approved domestic investment projects (Rp4,237 billion)
	%	%
Agriculture, forestry, fishing	10.3	18.0
Mining, quarrying	15.7	2.9
Manufacturing	65.9	67.1
Construction	1.0	0.4
Wholesale and retail trade	0.1	0.02
Restaurants and hotels	2.4	2.3
Transport, storage, communication	1.5	4.3
Financing, insurance, real estate, business services	2.8	4.4
Community, social and personal services	0.3	0.5

Source :- Investment Co-ordinating Board

Domestic investment to the end of March 1980 was at 80% of the level of foreign investment. However, domestic investment was spread over 3,384 projects by comparison with only 786 projects which had foreign investment. Average foreign investment was US$ 10.7 million per project, and average domestic investment was US$ 2.0 million.

Table 69 - Selected manufacturing industries by persons engaged, number of establishments, and employment costs

	Number of establishments	Employees	Unpaid workers	Employment costs(Rpmillion)
Food, beverage, tobacco manufacture	2,498	289,519	2,462	63,945
Textiles, leather	2,218	221,152	2,616	49,443
Wood, wood products	637	47,403	420	14,809
Paper, paper products	345	25,948	107	10,561
Chemical, rubber, plastic products	799	91,996	353	41,509
Other non-metallic mineral products	624	37,721	474	14,336
Basic iron, steel industry	17	3,978		1,725
Iron and steel machinery, equipment	735	91,706	420	46,512
Other manufacturing industries	82	4,777	70	1,080

Source :- Annual Survey of Large and Medium Manufacturing
Establishments - 1978

In the manufacturing sector most people are employed in the food, beverage and tobacco area although employment costs were lowest in 1978 at about US$ 353 per employee per annum. The second lowest cost per employee was US$ 358 in the textiles, leather industries.

At the other extreme companies manufacturing iron and steel machinery and equipment had annual per capita employee costs of US$ 812 while the equivalent figure for the chemical, rubber and plastic product industries was US$ 722.

Table 70 - Selected manufacturing sectors by value added
(Rp billion)

	Value of gross output	Input costs	Value added at market prices	Indirect taxes	Value added at factor cost
Food manufacturing	586	409	177	12	165
Beverage industries	39	16	23	11	12
Tobacco manufacturers	616	302	314	150	164
Textiles	443	311	132	4	128
Wearing apparel - non-footwear	7	4	3	*	3
Leather products - non-footwear	12	10	3	*	2
Footwear	15	7	7	1	7
Furniture and wood products	106	62	44	1	42
Paper and paper products	44	25	19	1	18
Printing and publishing	36	19	17	1	16
Chemicals and chemical products	283	144	138	6	133
Rubber products	261	198	63	6	57
Plastic products nec	35	22	13	1	12
Pottery and china	4	2	2	*	2
Glass and glass products	33	12	21	1	20
Other non-metallic mineral products	117	41	75	3	72
Basic iron and steel	24	19	5	1	5
Fabricated metal products	124	91	33	4	29
Machinery - non-electrical	33	14	18	1	17
Electrical machinery and appliances	155	101	54	5	49
Transport equipment	149	95	54	4	50
Professional, scientific, photographic	2	1	1	*	1
Other manufacturing industries	14	10	3	1	2
Total	3,139	1,917	1,222	214	1,008

Source :- Annual Survey of Large and Medium Manufacturing Establishments - 1978

DEVELOPMENT SECTORS

BKPM also publishes a useful 'Guide for Investors' which describes existing areas of activity and points out areas of investment potential. Although these are not all industrial areas per se, there are implications for related industrial production. The 1980 publication provides information for the following areas of development. Some illustrative statistics are included here but the publication merits direct reference.

Agriculture and * :- About one third of Indonesia's total land
fishing area is suitable for agriculture - only about 12% is currently cultivated. It is a top Government priority to develop the agricultural sector. There is seen to be enormous potential in such crops as rice, palm oil, sugar cane, rubber, coffee and tea. Indonesia also has abundant fish stocks -(the 1.5 million metric tons caught in 1977 was put at less than 20% of potential production). Currently 40,000 tons of shrimps are shipped overseas - 95% to Japan.

Forestry :- Indonesia has about 300 million acres of tropical forest - the richest timber resources in Southeast Asia. Paradoxically, it imports more than 80% of the paper needed for domestic consumption. Current (1980) approved investment projects total US$1.3 billion (about half foreign).

* Agriculture is dealt with in more detail in the next chapter.

Petroleum   :-   Pertamina has exclusive rights in the industry but operates 50-50 joint operation arrangements in production and exploration. Reserves are put at more than 50 billion barrels. Natural gas is seen as a high area of potential.

Mining   :-   Only 10% of the land area has been thoroughly surveyed but already there are known to be substantial mineral deposits of coal, bauxite, copper, iron and manganese. With the exception of coal and gold almost all mineral production is exported.

Fertilizer   :-   Indonesia's abundant natural gas is important to fertilizer production and export potential. Domestic consumption of fertilizer is estimated at 1980 to be rising by 15% per annum. In FY 1978/79 1.4 million tons were produced - 41% up on the previous year.

Petrochemicals   :-   At 1980 only one petrochemical plant was operating with a production capacity of 20,000 tons annually, although several others were under construction.

Pharmaceuticals   :-   1980 investment in this fast growing industry is estimated at US$100 million :- about two-thirds foreign. The industry at present mainly imports raw materials for batch processing and tablets rather than originating formulae. 1978 consumption is estimated at US$350 million (95% from local production) with a current growth rate of 15% in production.

Cement	:-	Fast growth in the industry led to the export of excess for the first time in 1978/79. There were 7 major plants at the end of FY 1978/79 with a total capacity of 7 million tons a year. Cement production grew 24% to 3.6 million tons in FY 1978/79. The Government is keen to develop this as an export commodity.

Cement :- Fast growth in the industry led to the export of excess for the first time in 1978/79. There were 7 major plants at the end of FY 1978/79 with a total capacity of 7 million tons a year. Cement production grew 24% to 3.6 million tons in FY 1978/79. The Government is keen to develop this as an export commodity.

Textiles :- Indonesia's oldest and largest manufacturing activity and an area of high developmental priority. By 1977 production had doubled over the previous eight years. In FY 1978/79 production of yarn increased by 32.7% and fabric by 50%. By 1977 industry approved investment was approximately US$1 billion. The textile industry will continue to be a heavy importer of raw materials and machinery.

Steel :- The estimated need for steel products such as bars, rods, wire, tubes at the end of 1980 is 1.7 million tons with demand increasing at about 11% per annum thereafter. At the end of 1977 there were 74 mostly small-scale plants. However, there has been a major development here in the form of PT Krakatau Steel which already has a bar and section mill and is planned to provide a steel plant in the Eighties with an annual capacity of 2.2 million tons.

| **Metal/machinery** | :- | Important industries with investment opportunities are the assembly of motor cars, trucks, motorcycles, agricultural machinery and component part production. Also diesel engine production and the manufacture of aluminium products (the Asahan aluminium smelter project is scheduled to start producing in 1982 at 75,000 tons per annum and reach full capacity of 225,000 tons by 1984). |
| **Food and food processing** | :- | At 1980 these industries were employing more than 600,000 people. With the relatively large increases in per capita GNP and hence purchasing power these are thought likely to be high growth areas. Industry standards are being improved with the help of Government capital. |

PETROLEUM

Petroleum is vital to the economy of Indonesia. In 1978 production averaged 1.63 million barrels a day making Indonesia the fourteenth largest oil producer in the world, the seventh largest among OPEC members and the second largest in the Asia Pacific region after China. In 1979 production fell by 3% to 1.59 million barrels a day. The value of oil and gas exports (net of expenditure on oil imports and services) was US$4.0 billion for FY 1978/79.

Indonesia has been described as a whole region of oil but individual fields tend to be small. About two hundred separate oil fields were discovered during the Seventies. With the rise in oil prices at the end of the decade investment in oil exploration rose sharply with exploration expenditure in 1979 at US$361 million. Total reserves are estimated at more than 50 billion barrels.

Foreign investment in exploration and production is encouraged. Pertamina the State oil company - plans to continue sharing oil exploration ventures through production - sharing contracts with foreigncompanies. In 1979, Indonesia's total oil production of 580.4 million barrels, 48% was produced by three foreign oil companies operating under contract-of-work agreement. Crude oil from production-sharing contracts accounted for 47% of total production (up from 23% in 1974).

Natural gas production increased from 543 billion standard cubic feet in 1977 to 820 billion in 1978 and an estimated 975 billion for 1979. the growth was largely due to the completion of several major liquefied natural gas projects.

Table 71 - Selected mineral production by year

	1978	1979
Petroleum ('000 barrels)	596,698	580,447
Tin ore concentrate ('000 metric tons)	27	29
Copper ore concentrate ('000 metric tons)	181	189
Nickel ore ('000 metric tons)	1,207	1,552
Bauxite ('000 metric tons)	1,008	1,058
Coal ('000 metric tons)	264	279
Iron sand concentrate ('000 metric tons)	218	80
Gold (Kgs)	254	170
Silver (Kgs)	2,506	1,645

Source :- Department of Mining and Energy

8 Agriculture

DEVELOPMENT

As the dominant sector of the Indonesian economy, the Government has given agriculture high priority during the three 5-year plans. In Repelitas I and II agriculture took 21.7% and 19.1% of development expenditure and it is expected to receive 14% of development expenditure in Repelita III.

About 12% of Indonesia's 735,000 square miles is under cultivation and it is believed that a further 77,000 square miles can be cultivated in Sumatra and Kalimantan and that in total about a third of Indonesia can come under cultivation.

Agriculture is largely in the hands of small-holding farmers but there are about 2000 estates with an average size of 3000 acres. Although this is a small proportion of the cultivated land the estates account for not much less than half of cash crop production.

In 1978 agriculture (excluding forestry and fishing) accounted for 26.5% of Gross Domestic product and employed about 6 in every 10 workers.

The table below shows recent production of the main agricultural products and the planned growth of cash crops to the end of Repelita III.

Table 72 - Production of main agricultural products

	('000 tons)		
	1977	1978	1979
Food crops			
- Rice (milled)	15,876	17,598	17,940
- Cassava	12,488	12,902	13,330
- Corn	3,143	4,029	3,305
- Sweet potatoes	2,460	2,083	2,043
- Soyabeans	523	617	674
- Peanuts	409	446	418
Livestock			
- Meat	468	477	N.A.
- Eggs	131	146	N.A.
- Milk (million litres)	61	62	N.A.
Cash crops			
- Copra	1,518	1,540	1,830
- Cane sugar (refined)	1,086	1,130	2,430
- Rubber	838	885	921
- Palm oil	483	596	979
- Coffee	197	235	315
- Tea	76	83	97

Source :- Central Bureau of Statistics
Indonesia Development News - March 1980

In 1965 the Government introduced two agricultural programmes - BIMAS and INMAS, to promote rice production and increase farm income. The main objectives of BIMAS are to encourage the use of higher yielding rice seeds, fertilizer and insecticide and to expand irrigation facilities. These activities are supported with agricultural credits provided in kind (such as fertilizer) and cash. The INMAS programme is similar to BIMAS but for farms at a more advanced stage of development. In the 1978/79 wet season 9.1. milion acres were covered by these two programmes. The period 1970-78 has seen an increase in average yield from acreage under these programmes from 1.7 tons per acre to 1.8 tons per acre. Irrigation has been an area of considerable activity and remains a main priority. Repelita III plans for some 1,724,050 acres of irrigation systems in addition to 1,321,500 acres of tidal systems and the improvement of 1.5million acres of tertiary systems.

FOOD CROPS

Indonesia has such serious problems in trying to feed its population that virtually all food crops are for domestic consumption. Rice is the staple food and the most important commodity in the economy. Despite producing about 18 million tons of milled rice a year Indonesia is also the world's largest importer of rice.

In recent years the production growth has been variable falling behind consumption growth in 1975 to 1977 but improving by 11% in 1978 with good weather and fewer pest problems. In 1979 the production estimate was 17.94 million tons and consumption was put at 17.1 million tons. However, the production estimate did not account for seed retention and farmers' own consumption, put at about 10% of total production. The result has been that Indonesia has had to import 1.5 to 1.8 million tons of rice a year to cover the deficit and build buffer stocks. During the 1980/81 fiscal year Indonesia plans to import 1.75 million tons of rice mainly from Thailand.

This heavy reliance on imported rice is a situation the Government is keen to remedy. Rice is a relatively expensive foodstuff to be buying and can go short on world markets. In addition to increasing its own rice production Indonesia is encouraging production and consumption of other crops, particularly corn and cassava.

COMMERCIAL CROPS

The Government is encouraging foreign investors to develop plantation crops into the country's second largest foreign exchange earner (after petroleum and gas) by the end of Repelita III. By 1984 export earnings from plantation commodities are planned at US$2.5 billion per year and to achieve this the land area for plantations is being expanded by 1.3 million hectares. Planned production levels in 1984 are shown in the table above. At present the Government is considering new incentive schemes to bring in foreign investors.

Rubber has traditionally been the main agricultural export commodity :- almost all of the rubber produced is exported. Just over 30% of production in 1978 was from estates with the remainder from small-holdings. An extensive programme of rubber tree planting in the early Seventies will lead to crops maturing in the Eighties and give a solid boost to production.

While exports of rubber in 1979 totalled US$937 million, the second largest export crop was coffee at US$615 million. Coffee has become particularly important since the substantial rise in world prices that began in 1976. Export value has remained sensitive to world prices but production is planned to grow by a third during Repelita III.

The third largest export crop is palm oil (US$205 million in 1979). Palm oil has seen considerable growth during the Seventies, from export value of US$45 million in 1971. Indonesia is the world's second largest exporter of palm oil - after Malaysia. About 80% of production is exported.

Prior to World War II Indonesia was the world's largest sugar cane producer, but since then the industry has been seriously neglected. Production is now increasing again but it is almost entirely consumed domestically. Production costs are such that imported sugar still tends to be cheaper.

Tea is another crop where exports have been growing quickly (US$29 million in 1971 to US$84 million in 1979). Copra and pepper are the other main export crops both with an export value in 1979 in excess of US$40 million.

GOVERNMENT PRIORITIES

While the Government is committed to general development of the agricultural sector it has placed its highest priorities in the following areas :-

- increasing rice production to match rising needs,
- increasing the supply of milk, meat and eggs to upgrade average nutritional levels,
- improving small-holder farming techniques in order to match the quality and per acre yields of large estates,
- (with the other related main priority of the development of fishing)

9 External trade

Indonesia's trade picture is dominated by oil. The total trade balance for 1979 including oil showed a surplus of US$8.4 billion. Without oil the surplus was only US$0.3 billion (having previously been in deficit through the Seventies).

Table 73 - Balance of Trade (US$ billion)

	1976	1977	1978	1979
Balance of trade including oil	2,873.4	4,622.3	4,952.8	8,353.1
Balance of trade excluding oil	-2,693.0	-1,943.5	-1,906.0	+ 288.5

Source :- Central Bureau of Statistics

The sharp increase in the balance of trade figure for 1979 reflects the rise in the price of crude oil rather than increased production (production actually declined by 10%).

However, the latter part of the Seventies has seen an increase in exports of other main commodities.

Table 74 - Export growth in non-oil commodities

	Exports in US$ million FY 1978/9	% change FY 1974/5 - 1978/9
Wood	1,130	+ 84
Rubber	774	+ 82
Tin	324	+ 95
Palm oil	221	+ 20
Coffee	508	+452
Tobacco	58	+ 61
Tea	98	+ 96
Pepper	66	+200
Copra cake	34	+ 55

Source :- Central Bureau of Statistics

During the period of Repelita III (1979/80 FY to 1983/84 FY) net export earnings for non-oil commodities and manufactured goods are projected to increase by about 90% from US$4.0 billion to US$7.7 billion while earnings from oil and gas are projected to rise only 28%. An important element in developing non-oil exports is the National Agency for Export Development established in 1974 which acts both as an export liaison office and a supplier of information on export opportunities.

Indonesia's top six exports for 1979 were :-

	US$ million
- petroleum and derivatives	8,858
- wood	1,837
- rubber	937
- coffee	615
- tin	404
- palm oil	205

In terms of trading partners, Japan is the largest followed by the United States and Singapore. However, it should be borne in mind that there is suspected to be a good deal of unofficial trade - particularly with Singapore - which does not show up in official figures.

Table 75 - Distribution of total trade by country

	% of Total Trade	% Growth 1978-79
ASEAN	13.5	44.2
- Malaysia	0.4	137.5
- Thailand	1.1	115.4
- Philippines	0.9	-22.0
- Singapore	11.0	47.6
Japan	40.8	41.2
USA	18.4	10.6
Australia	1.8	27.0
Netherlands	2.3	3.6
West Germany	3.5	-2.5

Source :- Central Bureau of Statistics

The overall growth in trade between 1978 and 1979 was 24.3% and it can be seen above that this growth was disproportionately with ASEAN countries. ASEAN is of growing importance to Indonesia's trade particularly as the number of preferential trading arrangements increases. By April 1980 4,325 items had been approved for ASEAN tariff preferences.

Although Japan accounts for a large proportion of Indonesia's trade, the balance is heavily in Indonesia's favour because of Japan's heavy imports of crude oil. In 1979 77% of Indonesia's trade with Japan was exports to Japan. In 1979 the countries with the largest trade surplus with Indonesia were Thailand (rice) and England - both with surpluses in excess of US$100 million.

Despite its own oil resources, Indonesia's refining capacity is rather antiquated, with the result that it has to import refined petroleum to satisfy increasing domestic consumption. In 1979 petroleum and petroleum products were the country's main import commodity. Industrial and commercial machinery was the second largest specific import category, and increased in dollar terms over 1978 by 11.1%

Table 76 - Imports of Specific Commodities (1979)

	US$ million
Consumer	
- Milk, cream	38.5
- Rice	592.7
- Cereal Products	9.1
- Pharmaceutical preparations	52.7
- Cotton dyed and coloured	2.6
- Sewing machines	5.4
Raw materials and auxiliary	
- Cloves	68.1
- Chemicals	429.4
- Fertilizer	56.0
- Paper	71.2
- Weaving yarns of cotton	3.6
- Cement	17.2
- Iron and steel bars	78.8
- Petroleum and products	793.3
Capital goods	
- Iron or steel pipes	102.7
- Prime movers	174.4
- Internal combustion engines	50.9
- Industrial and commercial machines	759.7
- Motor cars	97.9
- Buses and trucks	21.4

Source :- Central Bureau of Statistics

Table 77 - Commodity exports by year (US$'000)

	1978	1979
Total	**11,643,175**	**15,590,144**
Live animals, animal products	189,097	233,024
Vegetable products	734,787	934,539
Animal and veg. fats and oils	214,650	223,100
Prepared food, beverages, spirits, vinegar, tobacco	160,015	192,335
Mineral products	8,087,305	10,314,947
Chemical products	59,325	63,591
Artificial resins, plastics, rubber and products	718,559	940,764
Leather, skins and products	24,576	43,781
Wood, cork, plaiting and products	1,023,841	1,850,091
Paper, paper board and products	233	5,061
Textiles and products	18,277	110,607
Footwear, headgear, umbrellas, human hair etc.	1,441	1,268
Stone, plastic, cement, glass articles	180	3,747
Precious stones and metals	1,656	3,056
Base metals and products	313,860	504,055
Machinery and electrical equipment	58,907	100,648
Vehicles and transport equipment	11,663	15,258
Optical, photographic, medical, musical	3,626	6,492
Ammunition and parts	1	2
Miscellaneous manufactured	1,820	3,097
Objets d'art	19,356	40,681

Source :- Central Bureau of Statistics

Table 78 - Commodity imports by year (US$'000)

	1978	1979
Total	**6,690,423**	**7,202,279**
Live animals, animal products	63,872	63,798
Vegetable products	803,539	878,916
Animal and veg. fats and oils	65,689	32,379
Prepared food, beverages, spirits, vinegar, tobacco	246,955	182,456
Mineral products	640,641	852,140
Chemical products	607,157	797,936
Artificial resins, plastics, rubber and products	223,116	299,307
Leather, skins and products	2,191	2,108
Wood, cork, plaiting and products	3,667	2,630
Paper, paper board and products	166,755	175,064
Textiles and products	350,083	421,693
Footwear, headgear, umbrellas, human hair etc.	7,828	3,595
Stone, plaster, cement, glass articles	53,648	51,943
Precious stones and metals	36,221	19,370
Base metals and products	827,893	950,479
Machinery and electrical equipment	1,597,822	1,651,665
Vehicles and transport equipment	819,073	619,277
Optical, photographic, medical, musical	112,396	138,236
Ammunition and parts	24,021	20,088
Miscellaneous manufactured	35,439	35,395
Objets d'art	2,417	3,804

Source :- Central Bureau of Statistics

10 Labour force

Apart from its abundant natural resources one of Indonesia's greatest assets is its people. The 1976 Labour Force Survey put the working population at 46.4 million and by the end of Repelita III (1984) this number is projected to grow to 54.5 million.

In common with the population at large the workforce is young. However, skilled workers are hard to come by and good quality upper/middle level management is also rare. The Indonesian Government cites low wage levels and speed in learning new skills as main advantages of its workforce. Employers counter that productivity tends to be low (when making regional comparisons), there are low educational levels among potential trainees and there is a background of bureaucratic red tape which also tends to slow production.

Nevertheless, the Government has put much emphasis in recent years on developing a skilled manpower pool. Against a background of increasing educational opportunities, thirteen vocational training centres have been established (at 1980) and 17 more are planned. Training covers skills such as metal and wood working, construction trades, electrical trades, administration and agricultural technology.

LABOUR FORCE PROFILE

Statistics from the 1976 Intercensal Survey provide information on the profile of the work force. In that survey the 'economically active' population was defined as those aged 10 years and above either working or looking for work. The economically active population was 61.3% of the total 10+ population and included 23.4% of the 10-14 age group and 55.5% of the 15-19 age group.

Outside the economically active group the main occupations were house-keeping 17.7% and attending school 14.4%. Among the 10-14s, 61.1% were attending school.

Within the economically active group 98.1% claimed to be working. Outside the economically active group are two sizeable sub-groups headed 'thought no work available' (1.2 million) and 'others' (4.3 million, mainly at the young and old extremes). Unemployment would be somewhere between 2% and 12% depending on which categories are included in the definition.

Table 79 - Activity* of population aged 10 years and over

	Total Population	Economically active	('000s) Working	House-Keeping	Attending School	Others/ not stated
Age :-						
10 - 14	15,859	3,717	3,420	1,041	9,682	1,419
15 - 19	13,530	7,506	6,872	2,350	2,667	1,007
20 - 24	9,882	6,678	6,147	2,386	409	409
25 - 29	8,282	5,903	5,660	2,184	59	136
30 - 39	15,749	12,017	11,649	3,564	10	158
40 - 49	11,945	9,573	9,266	2,125	*	247
50 - 59	7,446	5,653	5,405	1,239	2	552
60+	6,131	3,431	3,156	870	2	1,828

Excludes certain main rural areas of East Nusatenggara, Maluku and Irian Jaya (and also not-stateds).

* Primary activity during last week of 1976
    Source :- Central Bureau of Statistics - 1976 Intercensal Survey.

Agriculture accounted for two thirds of the working population with trade and service industries such as tourism the other main employment categories. Women accounted for 38.6% of all working people and were found disproportionately in the manufacturing and trade categories.

Table 80 - Industry of working population by sex

	Total Employed Population	Male	Female
	%	%	%
Employed in:-			
- Agriculture	66.0	65.1	67.3
- Mining	0.1	0.1	*
- Manufacturing	6.7	5.7	8.1
- Electricity	0.1	0.1	*
- Construction	2.1	3.3	0.1
- Trade	11.7	9.9	14.6
- Transportation	2.1	3.3	0.1
- Finance	0.1	0.2	0.1
- Services	9.6	10.8	7.9
- Others	1.6	1.5	1.8

Source :- Central Bureau of Statistics - 1976 Intercensal survey

The Government is aiming to provide substantial employment opportunities with its urban and rural works programme and planned migration. With development in the industrial sector the Government estimates that by the end of Repelita III (1984) the agricultural sector will have 56% of the workforce and the industry sector 11%.

There is some variability in the workforce profile through the year with many agricultural workers migrating to urban areas between harvests.

WAGES

There is a statutory minimum wage in the private sector decided by the Minister of Labour and Transmigration. In 1979 this was about US$0.7 per 8 hour day for unskilled labour and about US$4.00 per day for the relatively hard to find skilled labour.

Wages vary quite considerably across the islands and regions from low points in the heavily populated rural areas of Java to high points in the less populated islands of Sumatra, Sulawesi, Irian Jaya and Kalimantan.

The figures in the tables below will give an indication of earnings per year in Jakarta.

Table 81 – Annual earnings for various occupation groups in Jakarta

	Earnings per annum (US$)
Primary school teacher	1,400
Bus driver	1,200
Automobile mechanic	1,400
Construction worker	1,000
Tool maker	1,200
Cook	3,200
Technical department manager (100 employees+)	5,000
Electrical engineer (graduate)	3,700
Bank teller	1,900
Secretary	2,900
Saleswoman (department store)	700
Textile worker (semi/unskilled female)	400

* Net of tax and social insurance contributions paid by employers.

Source :- Union Bank of Switzerland -'Prices and Earnings around the Globe' 1979/80

TRADES UNIONS

As a signatory of Convention No.98 of the International Labour Organis-
ation, Indonesia guarantees workers the right to form unions and
bargain collectively with employers. Indonesia has one official labour
federation - the FBSI - to which unions must be affiliated to be
officially recognised. About 40% of the workforce is nominally
unionized, but only 5% to 10% are thought to be active. However, all
strikes are currently banned by the Government.

11 Media and advertising

MEDIA USAGE

The main source of information on media usage in Indonesia is the annual 'Media Index Survey' carried out by In-Search Data. Tables in this chapter have been taken from the 1979 survey which took place in the last 4 months of that year. The sample comprised 12,014 adults rigorously selected (by probability sampling method) to represent 10 major cities.

Television is Government owned :- Televisi Republic Indonesia providing the only television network which covers the whole country. However, there are Government controlled local stations which produce two hours of local programmes per night. On an average day about half the adult urban population watch TV but it is relatively rare for viewers to watch more than two hours a day. With the penetration of TV sets still quite low (about 4 in 10 urban homes) an interesting feature of viewing is that much of it occurs in someone else's home.

Table 82 - Place of TV viewing

	Total adults (10 cities)
('000s)	8,787
	%
watch TV	87
- Usually watch in own home	48
- friends/relatives' home	38
- public place	1

Source :- In-Search Media Index Survey - 1979

TV viewing is at its highest in the better-off cities of Sumatra and at its lowest in the Javanese cities of Malang and Semarang (where the population is somewhat older and less well-off).

Until the end of March 1981 TV commercials occured in two blocks of half an hour - early (6.30-7.00pm) and one later evening (8.30-9.00pm). From April 1981 all TV advertising was banned (see below). While they were on, TV commercials were in effect programmes in their own right and 7% of all viewers specifically named them as their favourite programme (10% of female viewers). Of the other programme types plays are the most popular with women, news programmes most popular with men. Music is the third most liked programme type among all viewers followed by sport and films (imported rather than local). The Government appears to appreciate the power of Television in shaping opinion and TV has a solid component of religious and development oriented programmes. There is not much difference in the incidence of viewing between men and women but viewing declines sharply with those aged 40 or over. Jakarta serves as an example :-

Table 83 - Average daily TV viewing by sex and age (Jakarta)

	Total Adults	Male	Female	15-19	20-29	30-39	40+
('000s)	3,750	1,895	1,855	710	1,348	804	888
	%	%	%	%	%	%	%
Watched TV yesterday	45	47	43	55	47	41	36

Source :- In-Search Media Index Survey - 1979

The incidence of yesterday TV viewing in Jakarta was estimated at 43% of adults in the equivalent In-Search survey for 1977.

The Government also has a **radio** network - Radio Republic Indonesia (RRI)- but there are many small radio stations that accept advertising. The 1979 Media Index Survey located respondents who had listened to 64 stations in Jakarta, 35 in Surabaya, 36 in Medan, 23 in Jogyakarta, 52 Bandung, 25 in Palembang, 24 in Solo, 32 in Semarang, 19 in Malang and 34 in Ujung Pandang.

In urban areas the incidence of radio listening on an average day is higher for men (45%) than women (38%). In terms of age, radio listening peaks with the 15-29 year olds. The demographic breakdown of radio listening for Jakarta is as follows:-

Table 84 - Average daily radio listening by sex and age (Jakarta)

	Total Adults	Male	Female	15-19	20-29	30-39	40+
('000s)	3,750	1,895	1,855	710	1,348	804	888
	%	%	%	%	%	%	%
Listened to radio yesterday	41	47	35	55	47	35	25

Source :- In-Search Media Index Survey - 1979

In-Search estimates that the incidence of radio listening in Jakarta declined from 49% in 1977 to 41% in 1979.

Radio listening does not appear to be a function of household expenditure level and with growing numbers of young people the gross audience size should increase steadily in the short term.

At the end of 1979 8% of adults in the 10 cities had visited the **cinema** in the past week - (19% in the past two weeks). With the exception of Ujung Pandang where cinema going is less frequent there was little difference between the other cities.

Cinema has been a particularly important advertising medium in Indonesia because advertising opportunities on TV and Press have been limited. However, although its cover is fairly broad over a two week time period the profile of cinema visitors is youthful and predominantly male. Cigarette manufacturers who find it hard to use budgets elsewhere are very heavy users of cinema advertising.

Table 85 - Average weekly and fortnightly cinema going by sex and age (Jakarta)

	Total Adults	Male	Female	15-19	20-29	30-39	40+
('000s)	3,750	1,895	1,855	710	1,348	804	888
Attended cinema	%	%	%	%	%	%	%
- in past week	8	9	6	13	11	4	1
- in past 2 weeks	19	23	14	82	25	11	4

Source :- In-Search Media Index Survey - 1979

The incidence of cinema going in Jakarta was stable between 1977 and 1979

There are very many **newspapers** in Indonesia, with both national and local circulations. The 1979 In-Search Media Index Survey included (and consquently has readership figures for) the following 33 daily publications

Angkatan Bersenjata	Harian Gala	Media Indonesia
Analisa	Harian Indonesia	Mimbar Umum
Bawakareng	Indonesian Observer	Merdeka
Berita Buana	The Indonesia Times	Mimbar Karya
Berita Nasional	Jawa Pos	Pedoman Rakyat
Berita Yudha	Kedaulatan Rakyat	Pelita
Business News	Kompas	Pikiran Rakyat

Pos Kota	Suara Merdeka
Pos Sore	Suara Rakyat Semesta
Republik	Sumatra Express
Sinar Harapan	Surabaya Post
Sinar Indonesia Baru	Tegas
Suara Karya	Waspada

Education and literacy are obviously important factors in determining levels of newspaper readership. On an average day at the end of 1979 48% of men but only 29% of women read a newspaper in the 10 main cities. The figures below serve to indicate that age is not such an important discriminator of newspaper readers.

Table 86 - Average daily readership of newspapers by sex and age (Jakarta)

	Total Adults	Male	Female	15-19	20-29	30-39	40+
('000s)	3,750	1,895	1,855	710	1,348	804	888
	%	%	%	%	%	%	%
Read daily newspaper yesterday	42	52	32	47	45	46	31

Source :- In-Search Media Index Survey - 1979

Income - already seen to be a correlate of education and literacy - is strongly related to newspaper readership. In 1979, 70% of adults from homes in Jakarta spending more than Rp 75,000 per month were average issue newspaper readers :- only 22% of those from homes spending less than Rp 30,000 were.

Daily newspaper reading in Jakarta was marginally down in 1979 from 46% in 1977.

Across the 10 cities Kompas is the leading daily newspaper but there are important regional variations so that Pos Kota leads in Jakarta, Pikiran Rakyat in Bandung, Suara Merdeka in Semarang and Solo, Surabaya Post in Surabaya and Analisa in Medan. Elsewhere Kompas leads.

Magazine content is varied but as a general category women are more important in the readership profile than they are with newspapers. Across the 10 cities Kompas Minggu (predominantly male) leads the weeklies followed by Bobo (predominantly female). The fortnightlies are dominated by the mainly female magazines Femina, Gadis, Kartini (although they all have solid male readerships) with Intisari the main monthly. Jakarta is again taken to reflect the age and sex differences in magazine readership.

Table 87 – Readership of leading weeklies, fortnightlies and monthlies by sex and age (Jakarta)

	Total Adults	Male	Female	15-19	20-29	30-39	40+
('000s)	3,750	1,895	1,855	710	1,348	804	888
	%	%	%	%	%	%	%
Read in past week							
- Kompas Minggu	8	10	6	8	10	8	5
- Bobo	4	3	6	10	3	6	1
Read in past two weeks							
- Femina	7	5	9	7	9	7	5
- Gadis	7	4	9	15	7	3	3
- Kartini	7	5	10	7	8	9	5
Read in past 4 weeks							
- Intisari	7	9	5	10	8	6	5

Source :- In-Search Media Index Survey - 1979

Table 88 – Readership of newspapers and magazines by city (10 cities)

	Total Adults	Jakar -ta	Ban- dung	Sema- rang	Solo	Jogya- karta	Sura- baya	Malang	Medan	Palem -bang	Ujung Pandang
('000s)	8,787	3,753	795	599	292	255	1,323	291	675	407	397
	%	%	%	%	%	%	%	%	%	%	%
Read daily newspapers yesterday	37	42	39	34	19	48	32	20	52	18	32
Read weekly magazines in past week	20	23	22	11	16	21	19	17	13	17	11
Read fortnightly magazines in past week	18	18	22	12	16	22	20	15	17	13	15
Read monthly magazines in past month	9	9	14	5	9	12	11	9	6	6	6

Source :- In-Search Media Index Survey - 1979

Table 89 - Cinema, TV, radio - attendance, viewing, listening by city (10 cities)

	Total Adults	Jakar -ta	Ban- dung	Sema- rang	Solo	Jogya- karta	Sura- baya	Malang	Medan	Palem -bang	Ujung Pandang
('000s)	8,787	3,753	795	599	292	255	1,323	291	675	407	397
	%	%	%	%	%	%	%	%	%	%	%
Attended cinema in past week	8	8	8	8	8	7	9	8	9	7	3
Watched TV yesterday	45	45	49	33	40	44	47	31	52	45	46
- watch more than 2 hours a day on average	11	13	10	9	8	9	10	6	9	7	9
Listened to radio yesterday	41	41	52	35	42	55	41	33	41	36	40

Source :- In-Search Media Index Survey - 1979

Table 90 - Leading * daily newspapers by city (10 cities)

	Total Adults	Jakar -ta	Ban- dung	Sema- rang	Solo	Jogya- karta	Sura- baya	Malang	Medan	Palem -bang	Ujung Pandang
('000s)	8,787	3,753	795	599	292	255	1,323	291	675	407	397
	%	%	%	%	%	%	%	%	%	%	%
Read yesterday :-	8	8	8	8	8	7	9	8	9	7	3
- Kompas	12	17	16	6	7	14	6	10	3	10	8
- Pos Kota	9	19	2	*		*	1	*	*	*	*
- Sinar Harapan	7	12	3	2	4	4	3	3	2	2	2
- Surabaya Post	4	5					*	25	3		
- Merdeka	3	5	2	1	2	1	3	5	*	8	1
- Pikiran Rakyat	3	*	29								
- Suara Merdeka	3			32	9	2					
- Berita Buana	2	4	1	*		1	1	1	*	3	1
- Analisa	2								26		
- Sinar Indonesian Baru	2								23	*	

* Includes newspapers with an estimated average issue readership in excess of 150,000 for the 10 cities.

Source :- In-Search Media Index Survey - 1979

Table 91 - Leading * magazines by city (10 cities)

	Total Adults	Jakar -ta	Ban- dung	Sema- rang	Solo	Jogya- karta	Sura- baya	Malang	Medan	Palem -bang	Ujung Pandang
('000s)	8,787	3,753	795	599	292	255	1,323	291	675	407	397
	%	%	%	%	%	%	%	%	%	%	%
Weeklies:-											
Read in past week											
- Kompas Minggu	6	8	12	4	4	7	2	3	1	3	2
- Bobo	5	5	6	3	3	7	5	4	4	3	2
- Sinar Marapan Minggu	4	7	2	1	2	4	2	2	1	1	1
- Tempo	3	4	5	2	1	4	4	2	2	2	2
- DR	3	2	3	2	3	2	5	4	4	7	2
- Buana Minggu	3	5	2	*	*	2	2	2	*	3	*
Fortnightlies:-											
Read in past 2 weeks											
- Femina	8	7	11	6	5	11	9	7	7	4	8
- Gadis	7	7	9	5	6	9	10	7	7	6	5
- Kartini	7	8	9	7	7	10	8	5	5	4	6
- Sport Otak	2	2	3	1	1	2	2	1	2	2	2
Monthlies:-											
Read in past 4 weeks											
- Intisari	7	7	11	4	7	10	8	8	5	5	5

* Includes publications with an estimated average issue readership in excess of 150,000 for the 10 cities

Source :- In-Search Media Index Survey - 1979

Table 92 - Most popular types of TV programme (10 cities)

	Total adults (10 cities)	
	('000s) 8,787	
	%	
Type of TV programme watched most		
- Fragmen/Sandiwara	22	(Plays)
- Mana Suka Siaran Niaga	6	(Commercials)
- Berita Nusantara/Siaran Berita/Dunia DLM Berita	16	(New, current affairs)
- Siaran Olah Raga	8	(Sports)
- Siaran Pandangan Mata	1	(Direct broadcasts)
- Musik	11	(Music - pop,jazz or classical)
- Film Import	6	(Imported films)
- Film Indonesia	1	(Indonesian films)
- Film Kartun	1	(Cartoons)
- Mimbar Agama/Mimbar Kepercayaan	3	(Religious forum)
- Others	9	
- None/Don't know	1	
- Never watch TV	13	

Source :- In-Search Media Index Survey - 1979

ADVERTISING RATES AND RESTRICTIONS

In general the buying of advertising in Indonesia is a rather 'messy' business. Posters are a good example of this. There are plenty of sites and posters are in fact prevalent. The approximate cost is Rp80 per square metre per day: (on top of which Government tax must be paid). However, there is no central buying agency and site rates are very negotiable. This not only creates an administrative problem but a number of people are likely to be involved in the complete arrangement (area head man, site owner, maintenance etc) and unpredictable sums of 'unofficial' money are likely to have to change hands. For these reasons advertising agencies are not keen to handle poster advertising.

Government tax also applies to liveried vans and point of sale material although not to calenders.

The situation has been further confused by the recent ban on all TV advertising. This action has ostensibly been taken to minimise the spread of city habits to the countryside and to protect traditional cultural behaviour. At the same time, the forthcoming elections may have been at the back of the Government's mind and it has been suggested that this is not a time for raising consumer expectations too high. However advertising restrictions have occurred before and have been lifted and for this reason some illustrative discussion of TV advertising, as it was, is included in the following paragraphs.

Television was the most cost effective medium for Indonesia's mass markets but here there was a serious problem of availability. There were two half hour periods of advertising per day :- one from 6.30-7-00pm for local advertising and one from 8.30-9.00pm for national advertising. However, any single advertiser was limited to only 4 spots per month. The timing and position of these spots could be controlled.

A limited number of programme sponsorships were available but were in high demand and consequently almost impossible to break into - despite high sponsorship fees.

Table 93 - Examples of advertising rates - TV

		30 secs	60 secs (Rps)
Jakarta			
- Siaran Niaga I	(6.30-7.00pm)	214,500	330,000
- Siaran Niaga II	(8.30-9.00pm)	386,100	594,000
Surabaya	(6.30-7.00pm)	107,250	165,000
Medan	"	78,000	120,000
Jogyakarta	"	35,100	54,000
Palembang	"	58,500	90,000

Source :- In-Search Data

There have been problems with the execution of TV advertising. In some cases a local TV station may have put out its own local advertising in the national time segment to the obvious detriment of someone who believed he had bought that time nationally. Since the market was very much a seller's one, it was not of much use - and could be harmful - to complain.

The sequence for obtaining approval for TV advertising could also be troublesome. The first step was to obtain storyboard (provisional) approval from the Censor Board and then to return for approval of the finished advertising. However, TVRI still had the final say on the finished work and an expensive advertising creation may have been ruled out at this stage even with Censor Board approval.

The TV station did not normally accept advertising using superlatives or for cigarettes, although it may have bent its rules if it was temporarily short of bookings. With no shortage of takers for advertising time the TV station attitude was felt to have been a cautious one to avoid the risk of public criticism.

Newspapers have benefited from the shortage and now lack of TV advertising time. However, recent regulations (considered to be a Government pre-election show of strength) have reduced them to a maximum of 12 pages and 30% advertising. The result has been heavy price increases. Similar restrictions apply to magazines but, as with newspapers, they have heavy forward bookings.

Table 94 - Examples of advertising rates - newspapers

	Per millimetre/column (Rps)
Jakarta	
Kompas	2,000
Sinar Harapan	1,500
Berita Buana	1,000
Pos Kota	1,000
Merdeka	1,200
Suara Karya	1,000
Bandung	
Pikiran Rakyat	1,350
Semarang	
Suara Merdeka	1,000
Surabaya	
Surabaya Post	1,000
Medan	
Analisa	500
Mimbar Umum	500
Sinar Indonesia Baru	500

Source :- In-Search Data

Table 95 - Examples of advertising rates - magazines

	Full page colour ('000 Rps)
Tempo	1,200
Intrisani	1,375
Femina	2,250
Kartini	1,400
Gadis	875
Bobo	600
Aktuil	500
Selecta	550

Source :- In-Search Data

Radio (with its numerous local stations) and cinema both present problems of booking and fulfilment. There is no central agency and deals are made on an individual basis. Advertisers generally do not expect complete fulfilment but hope that it is closer to 80% than 30%. There are implications for negotiation here in that while a lower rate may be negotiated this may subsequently lead to lower fulfilment.

Table 96 - Examples of advertising rates - radio

	Rps per second (maximum 60)
Jakarta	20-25
Bandung	15-20
Semarang	15-20
Surabaya	15-20
Jogyakarta	15-20
Medan	10-15
Palembang	5-10

Source :- In-Search Data

Despite these booking difficulties many of the larger companies find it hard to spend their budgets and find themselves forced into radio and cinema - a situation which tends to reinforce the media owner's hand.

Table 97 - Examples of advertising rates - cinema

Rps per week (approximately 21 showings)

Leading cinemas in

Jakarta -	Jakarta Theatre	125,000
	President	100,000
	Jayakarta	100,000
	Plaza	125,000
Bandung -	Kusantara	60,000
	Paramount	85,000
	Majestic	30,000
Semarang		30,000 - 45,000
Medan		10,000 - 15,000
Surabaya		40,000 - 50,000
Palembang		15,000 - 25,000
Solo		15,000 - 20,000
Smaller towns' cinemas (e.g. Sukabumi, Kuningan)		10,000 - 12,500

Source :- In-Search Data

Despite the size and potential of Indonesia's consumer markets its total and per capita advertising expenditure vis a vis the other countries of Asia Pacific is extremely low.

Table 98 – Advertising expenditure in the countries of Asia-Pacific (1978)

	Total annual expenditure (US$ million)	Expenditure per head of population (US$)
Japan	5,604	49.1
Australia	1,145	81.2
South Korea	277	7.6
Hong Kong	95	20.7
New Zealand	91	28.3
Thailand	86	1.9
Taiwan	86	5.0
Philippines	77	1.7
Indonesia	**57**	**0.4**
Malaysia	55	4.4
Singapore	51	21.9

Source :- Survey Research Singapore (Pte) Ltd.

12 Retail trade

There are no definitive statistics on the number and type of retail establishments in Indonesia. However, a number of general observations can be made about the retail set up.

The normal procedure (required by law) for a company distributing goods in Indonesia is to go through a local distributor. This tends to lead to a loss of control with the principal quickly losing touch of where his products are, and often unable to obtain accurate distribution feedback from the distributor. The distributing agent will send the goods out through his channels but there may well be weak regions which he covers up. He may also dump stock into the Jakarta Wholesale market in China-Town from where distribution control is completely lost.

Some companies use teams of 'merchandisers' who do not sell but may pass on orders. Given the uneven distribution that occurs, there is a valuable role for merchandisers to play in helping to check and build distribution cover. An alternative is to supply direct to a number of regional distributors to increase the degree of control.

Retailers frequently appear to be working off minimal or even zero margins in Indonesia. One hypothesized reason for this is that retailers are capitalising on the credit period they are allowed and making money from short term loans of the cash they receive. This phenomenon is found elsewhere in Asia. An alternative hypothesis which has been put forward for the bottled drinks markets is that the retailer will take his margin out of the deposit allowance. Additionally, in North Sumatra it has been suggested that beer bottles are being put into soy sauce factories (which has a variety of bottles) for 2 or 3 months before returning to the beer system :- again the retailer makes his margin from the pack rather than the product.

Retailers who find themselves liquid in the short term may well specu-
late, it would not be surprising to find a retailer stocking up very
heavily on say a cough product knowing he will have his market at the
change of season. Sweetened condensed milk is seen as another good
investment product. Certain companies appear to enjoy the retailers'
confidence and find it easier to get products accepted - Unilever
products, for example, are considered to be 'safe' by retailers.

Because of their general lack of control of the distribution system,
principals are reluctant to involve themselves in researching it. The
system tends to be perpetuated where overseas companies put in managers
for short periods :- they know that this is not a nut they can hope to
crack in just the one or two years between settling in and preparing to
leave. Furthermore, remedial action may lead a disgruntled distributor
to cause severe problems.

The paragraphs below describe the main types of retail outlet. In the
absence of hard data on numbers within type of outlet some proport-
ionate guesstimates are included to provide at least an indication.

There are some 20 to 25 large **supermarkets** in Jakarta with two main
chains - Galael and Hero. There has been some Government reaction
against supermarket development on the grounds that it is against the
small shopkeepers' interests. It so far appears that shoppers are
tending to shop lightly at supermarkets. There is a degree of
curiosity (they mainly sell imported goods) and they are comfortable
places to visit out of Jakarta's heat. A few shops outside Jakarta are
calling themselves 'supermarkets' but more because this is seen to be a
vogue term than that they really are so.

The next largest shop is known as a **'P and D'** (from the Dutch for
provisions and drugs) which sells mainly food provisions and usually
alcoholic beverages. Relatively spacious with shelves around, the
shopkeeper is likely to package your goods up and a boy will carry it
to your car (if you're from one of the 5% of urban homes with one).
This is very much a minority shop type - perhaps 1% or 2% in urban
areas.

The **'toko'** is the most common type of shop and may be found in markets such as Jakarta's Block M (a covered conglomeration of hundreds of such shops, there are about 50 in Jakarta) or outside. The market toko would typically be about 3 metres in frontage by 2 metres in depth with a mixture of products stacked all around. This is where the ordinary family is most likely to do its shopping. It is virtually impossible even to guess at the proportion of 'toko's but they could comprise as much as 80% of fixed shops in urban areas.

The other main shop type is the **'warung'** which is a very small shop of a few square metres selling a mixture of bits and pieces - usually the essentials of life which are low unit cost and they know will sell. There could be some confusion between a non-market 'toko' and a 'warung'- the former would be more formal in the sense of just selling goods and closing at night while the latter would be more flexible with its hours and one might be able to eat or drink there.

There are very many hawkers of drinks, cakes, snacks etc. The numbers fluctuate with the season since many hawkers have come in from the rural areas between rice planting and harvest. There is a good deal of snack eating although main meals are usually taken at home.

13 Information sources

For a comprehensive listing of almost 200 sources of information on Indonesia the reader is referred to 'Sources of Asian Pacific Economic and Marketing Information' by Blauvelt and Durlacher (Gower Publishing Co. Ltd.).

Those concerned with Indonesia's consumer markets will find considerable value in **'The Indonesian Consumer'** (In-Search Data/Data Impact). In addition to comprehensive information from In-Search Data and published sources, a particular feature of this report is a large number of in-depth interviews with marketing personnel from top consumer goods companies. Information about The Indonesian Consumer is obtainable from The Asia Pacific Centre in London (address at front) or PT In-Search Data in Jakarta (address in next chapter).
Other key published sources are shown below.

PRINCIPAL SOURCES OF SOCIAL, ECONOMIC AND MARKET INFORMATION

Indonesia

Indonesia - A guide for Investors   Investment Coordinating Board

Indonesia - Economic Update 1980   National Development Information
                                                           Office

Indonesia Development News (monthly) National Development Information
                                                           Office

Monthly Statistical Bulletin	Central Bureau of Statistics
National Socio-economic Survey (1976)	Central Bureau of Statistics
List of Priority Scales for Fields of Foreign Investment	Investment Coordinating Board
Financial Institutions in Indonesia	Bank Indonesia
Statistical Data on Tourism-Jakarta	Jakarta Tourism Development Board
Java-Bali	APA Productions (HK) Ltd.

Regional

Bankers Handbook for Asia	Asian Finance Publications
The ASEAN Report	The Asian Wall Street Journal
The Asian Press and Media Directory	Syme Media Enterprises

14 Market research

RESEARCH FACILITIES

As with other Asian countries the standards of market research practice are rather variable. However, it is possible to obtain research of a very high standard, incorporating strictly performed probability sampling, careful questionnaire design and efficient analysis.

Both quantitative and qualitative facilities are available for most common techniques. Syndicated research for many consumer markets is available and frequently offers trend data over a number of years.

Fieldwork can be commissioned by itself from research agencies but there are no companies offering fieldwork only. A major fieldwork problem lies in the size of Indonesia and research buyers should check fieldwork control procedures and the checking system. It is unusual for fieldwork to go beyond the 6 major cities of Jakarta, Surabaya, Medan, Bandung, Palembang and Jogyakarta.

The incidence of telephone ownership is far too low for most survey purposes and can be a troublesome interviewing medium (in terms of making contact even with high income/business respondents).

Postal interviewing is not common for samples of the population at large for reasons of a sizeable illiterate minority. While personal interviewing costs remain low, postal interviewing is unlikely to grow other than for highly specialized sample groups.

Interviewing is normally carried out in Bahasa Indonesia and question-naire translation needs to be checked thoroughly - preferably using a systematic back-translation procedure.

Industrial research is very difficult to carry out even with large research budgets. The markets tend to be very fragmented, cooperation is poor and there are doubts about published statistics in view of the extent of tax avoidance.

Syndicated retail audits do not exist and the retail structure in Indonesia would make it extremely difficult to run one in the full sense of an audit. However, certain retail information can be collected (distribution checks, prices etc.).

Typical market research costs at January 1981 are :-

a) Probability Sample of 1000 housewives in Jakarta and Surabaya
   - 30 minute questionnaire - 150 tables and diagnostic report.
   US$22,000

b) 4 group discussions with sample comprising 20% of total adult population including a diagnostic report.
   US$4,500

c) 200 product test personal interviews in Jakarta - one call -
   50 tables and diagnostic report.
   US$7,500

MARKET RESEARCH COMPANIES

The following companies offer fairly comprehensive market research services:

> P.T. In-Search Data
> Jl. Nusa Indah No.9,Tomang
> Tromol Pos 3020
> Jakarta Barat
> Tel: 591729 Telex: 46331 Sahid JKT
> (Attention In-Search Data)

The Asia Pacific Centre
2-6 Camden High Street
London NW1 OJH

Tel: 01-388 5021   Telex 887560   BMRUK

AVAILABLE RESEARCH REPORTS

The leading supplier of syndicated market research data is **In-Search Data** and the following is the list of services and reports available for purchase from that company at the end of 1980. Brand information is available for most products. Further details and prices can be obtained from any **SRG** office, or from **The Asia Pacific Centre** in London.

MEDIA INDEX GENERAL REPORT

Demographic analysis, with audience duplication, of readers of newspapers and magazines, television viewers, radio and Rediffusion listeners, cinema goers. This report has been available each year for 15 years, and is the main tool of media planners in Indonesia, used by all major advertising agencies. Special analysis reports are also offered for individual media.

TARGET GROUP REPORTS

These reports define users of products, and provide demographic and media exposure analysis. Individual reports are available for each of the following products or services.

Beverages
Beer, Stout

Household
Insecticide(aerosol and liquid), Analgesics, Sanitary Napkins, Sweetened Condensed Milk, Toilet Soap, Toothpaste.

PROFILE AND INCIDENCE REPORT

Incidence of usage and purchase, demographic profile of users.

Beverages
Beer, Health Food Drinks, Soft Drinks, Stout.

Toiletries
Deodorant(aerosol, stick, roll-on, squeeze), After Shave, Body Lotion, Cologne/Perfume, Face Cream, Face Powder, Hair Conditioner, Hair Cream, Hair Spray, Lipstick, Powder Shampoo, Razor Blades, Talcum Powder.

Household
Insecticide(aerosol and liquid), Air Freshener, Analgesics, Bandages, Bar Soap, Butter, Margarine, Chewing Gum, Chocolate, Cooking Oil, Cough Drops, Cough Syrup, Cream Detergent, Floor Cleaner, Ice Cream, Jam, Jamu, Kecap, Mosquito Coils, Powder Detergent, Sanitary Napkins, Seasoning, Sweetened Condensed Milk, Sweets/Confectionery, Toilet Soap, Tonic Wine, Toothpaste, Vermicide, Vitamin Liquid, Vitamin Tablets.

Miscellaneous
Ball Point Pens, Dry Batteries.

ASIAN PROFILES

A major media and marketing survey of upper class men covering 8 capital cities in Southeast and East Asia (including Jakarta). The survey was carried out by SRG companies on behalf of Time, Newsweek International and Readers Digest Assoc. Far East Ltd, from any of whom information can be obtained.

Notes for the tables

- A 'household' is defined as a group of people who sleep under the same roof and normally eat together.

- An 'adult' is a person aged 15 years or over.

- Household 'expenditure' is the total monthly expenditure in the household as estimated by the survey respondent.

- Population estimates are those applicable at the time of the survey

- Percentages have been rounded and may not always add to 100% precisely.

- An asterisk in the body of a table means less than one half per cent. A blank space or dash means zero.

- An asterisk beside a year means the figures are preliminary for the year.

- The letters N.A. mean not available for this publication.

- The letters nec mean not elsewhere classified.

Index